The Humanistic Viewpoint in the Social Sciences

By
Henry Winthrop
University of South Florida

MSS Information Corporation
655 Madison Avenue, New York, N.Y. 10021

Library of Congress Cataloging in Publication Data

Winthrop, Henry.
    The humanistic viewpoint in the social sciences.

    1. Social sciences. I. Title.
H83.W534   300   72-8660
ISBN 0-8422-5062-X
ISBN 0-8422-0269-2 (pbk.)

CONTENTS

It has been common in our time to find the ideal of a value-free social science riding high. The present group of papers does not ask for the repudiation of this ideal. The papers found here, by contrast, seek to show only that there are areas and aspects of social science in which questions of value are germane and in which a humanistic outlook may be distinctly relevant.

In Part I we have presented two areas, related to education and culture, which provide examples of unsolved problems in social adaptation. One of these problems has to do with the sad and unique situation of those who are intellectually marginal in a complex society. The other tries to explore some of the consequences for education and culture that may be expected in a society undergoing extensive cybernation.

Part II recognizes that in the area of international relations both the method of experiment and the use of the scenario accompanied by quantitative analysis may prove of some value. The first paper of this section suggests an experimental procedure for achieving increased understanding between pairs of countries and, at the same time, a reduction of cultural alienation between them. The second seeks to show that if the have-nations were to agree to a reallocation of the planet's resources, in a spirit of brotherhood and social altruism, many difficulties of a complex nature would still arise -- some demographic, some centering about allowable but variable, national standards of living, some involving drastic social, economic and technological innovations, and many likely to be cataclysmic in nature.

In Part III we have made an effort to show that perspective on social problems and an appropriate posture for the social sciences are both difficult to achieve unless both theory and research are tempered by some sort of an orientation that lies outside of the questions of fact involved and the research methodologies employed. The first paper in this section seeks to justify the thesis that efforts at social reconstruction are fraught with potential failure when they are governed by a tacit picture of immutable ends to be achieved. The second paper contrasts the ideological approach with that of applied, social science. The ideological approach represents one example of what we mean by a tacit picture of immutable ends to be achieved although, of course, it frequently represents an example of an immutable interpretation of events, that is used as an intellectual strait-jacket. The technical approaches of applied, social science are seen as superior but are also recognized as wooden and undesirable if they are not fused throughout with a humanistic bias. The third paper attempts to indicate the ways in which the risk of losing perspective in historical analysis, may be softened and reduced through an existential outlook. By implication, the same softening and reduction may prove to be fringe benefits for work conducted in the other social sciences, when an existential outlook, properly understood, is adopted.

Part IV is concerned with exploring the effects of what psychologists call "the cognitive framework" upon the outlook and behavior of individuals and groups. The first, brief paper in this section discusses how the individual's framework of values will affect the range and levels of his awareness of the meaning of events. Today, as a result of the activities of Womens Lib, we would speak of methods for improving the quality of awareness as "consciousness-raising" techniques. The second paper is concerned with the spread of a humanist value-outlook and seeks to explore how sanguine or pessimistic we have a right to be, when we raise the 64 dollar question of whether there are educational methods which may implant or heighten the individual's felt sensitivity to social and moral values. The third paper of Part IV tries to show some of the consequences that flow for the human condition when a humanistic and existential sense of value is feeble or non-existent in the breasts of large numbers of men and women. In particular, it sets forth some of the causes and conditions that we, ourselves, generate, which enfeeble or prevent the development of an intensely but intelligently held value-outlook. These are causes and conditions that make unviable the adoption of a humanistic viewpoint in the social and behavioral sciences.

We hope that the present collection of material will give some support to the thesis that there is a place for the humanistic viewpoint in the social sciences. We hope further that this material will serve as a corrective to that narrowness of outlook in the social and behavioral sciences, which is so widespread today.

Henry Winthrop

Tragedy of intellectual marginality: its problems, tensions and pressures

The "intellectually underprivileged" may be defined *psychometrically* as those who possess I.Q.'s in the range of 70 to 89. Under the growing impact of automation, they may be defined *economically* as those who possess skills so marginal to the needs of the industrial sector that they are most easily automated. This deprives the intellectually underprivileged of their traditional job opportunities. They are the individuals who can profit least from academic training at the secondary school level. They cannot, therefore, go through the type of intellectual training needed for the professional skills that a college or university can supply. Nor do they have the capabilities required for completing the training needed for complex skills of a high order—skills so characteristic of many of the new occupations emerging in the West as a result of rapidly changing science and technology. The services they have traditionally supplied are so unspecialized that they cannot vie with people who are intellectually average (or better than average) and who can usually supply these same services more efficiently in a competitive job market.

The intellectually underprivileged are not to be confused with the mentally deficient. The latter require custodial care; the former are assumed everywhere to be capable of supporting and taking care of themselves. This assumption is increasingly being recognized as unrealistic in the United States. The industrial effects of "cybernation" (linkage of the computer with automatic, self-regulating machinery) is to withdraw their traditional job market from the intellectually underprivileged by ensuring that their unspecialized services can always be duplicated by a combination of electronic and mechanical slaves. Inasmuch as this group constitutes about 22.5

MENTAL HYGIENE, Oct. 1965, vol. 49, #4, 507-517.

per cent of our total population, concerns of common humanity, as well as considerations of an economic nature, dictate that we must do something to make meaningful for this group the democratic guarantee of the right to life, liberty and the pursuit of happiness.

America happens to be the first nation that will have to struggle with the problem of providing economic opportunities for the intellectually underprivileged while, at the same time, conferring upon them a sense of personal dignity and social value. Other advanced nations will eventually have to follow suit. If we ignore the right of the intellectually underprivileged to find an economic and social niche for themselves—or, worse still, if the Western community does nothing to provide that niche—their smoldering resentment may eventuate, in time, in behavior which might have to be christened "The Revolt Of The Low I.Q.'s."

Help to the intellectually underprivileged can be dealt with in a Utopian or a non-Utopian fashion. I wish to be fairly brief about the Utopian possibilities, but a fuller discussion of certain non-Utopian recommendations will be in order.

The Utopian Approach and Some of Its Needed Practical Modifications

Buber [1] defines the I-Thou relationship as one in which men try to understand the needs of others and minister to these needs regardless of whether or not they receive a return for their self-transcendent activities. Using a more wordly phraseology, we might say that under the sway of the I-Thou relationship men would apply the insurance principle to social and economic life, by underwriting adversity for one another and by distributing the burdens of misfortune, including misfortunes presumably brought about by Nature herself. To minister to the needs of others, our practical plans will have to be largely educational, economic and social in nature, but they will also have to include some genetic and medical proposals for the relief of the intellectually underprivileged. Such proposals can make sense only where genetic considerations have been shown to play a dominant role in the ineffective performance of *some* of the intellectually underprivileged. The assertion that there are hereditary determinants of intelligence is, at present, a controversial but not an unreasonable one. There seems to be strong evidence of genetic determinants in certain types of *mental deficiency*. Mental deficiency with genetic components has been found in such conditions as *phenylpyruvic oligophrenia, galactosemia* and certain cases of *cerebral palsy*. It does not seem unreasonable, therefore, to assume that genetic factors which might affect metabolic and neurophysiologic functioning (and thereby create conditions of mental deficiency) could also account for other cases of ineffectiveness in behavior and intellectual adjustment.

Such ineffectiveness in behavior and intellectual adjustment is precisely the condition that characterizes the intellectually underprivileged. Ineffective behavior upon the part of *some* members of this group may likewise be found to stem from hereditary considerations. To reason from genetic determinants in mental deficiency to genetic determinants in the limitations of the intellectually underprivileged is to reason by analogy. The seriousness with which this analogy is prosecuted will depend upon the degree to which future research will justify it. However, it should be recognized that (although they are in a minority) there are competent investigators like Penrose,[2] Kallman,[3] Cattell [4] and Hogben,[5] all of whom are convinced that intellectual capacity in the range of 70 to 89 I.Q. can be definitely shown to be associated with hereditary determinants. There would be nothing Utopian about genetic and medical planning aimed at the eventual reduction of the numbers of the intellectually underprivileged. Medical genetics, based upon that type of research in recent years that strives for the alleviation or elimination of ineffective intelligence, can be easily incorporated into practical planning.

The Utopian approach along these lines is something else again. Utopian expectations for the genetic improvement of man would, if successful, presumably result in the reduction or elimination of intellectual ineffectiveness. Such approaches have been described by Rostand,[6] Carrel,[7] Missenard,[8] du Noüy,[9] Simpson[10] and many others. Essentially, all of these Utopian approaches look toward an improvement of the human gene pool, so that (socially speaking) the day may come when (theoretically) there will be no intellectually underprivileged at all. We give such programs our blessing, but they are of no help in our current concern. For this reason we shall ignore any further discussion of the biologic, Utopian dream in this connection and turn, instead, to some non-Utopian proposals for dealing with the intellectually underprivileged. Our hope must be that some of these proposals may be feasible, and that resistance to many of them can be eliminated through public education.

Mechanization and Parkinson's Law

The biggest single factor threatening the economic future of the intellectually underprivileged is that the relatively simple unskilled and semiskilled services (which they have traditionally been able to supply) are precisely those most easily "cybernated" out of existence. The tendency of cybernation is to program a series of operations which are relatively simple when regarded separately. Cybernated production itself, however, demands programmers, industrial designers, repair and maintenance men and, in general, personnel peculiarly connected with computer-machine technology, regardless of whether production operations are of the open-loop or closed-loop type. This is in contrast to the *industrial mechanization* so characteristic of much of industrial production prior to the close of World War II. Here the emphasis was on an extreme division of labor and thus the exploitation of highly simplified skills—skills so simple, in fact, that many workers who were engaged in industry would be classifiable in the category of the intellectually underprivileged. However, even those newer skills that were not part of the industrial, behavioral repertoire of pre-World War II days can always be broken down into simple operations, based upon research on man-machine relationships.

Such a division of labor would, of course, open up a world of economic opportunity for the intellectually underprivileged. What I here suggest is the reopening of the economic frontier of mechanization to the intellectually underprivileged. But on what basis? No manufacturer employing the unskilled and semiskilled could compete in cost with an efficient producer who took advantage of all the savings in cost involved in cybernation and other forms of modern technology. To sell his products in the open market under conventional economic competition, he would have to bring his prices into line with those of competitive items. On this basis, he would be bankrupt in a short time. The only proper and ethical answer to this dilemma —if we may be allowed to mix morality and economics—is to make up the excess of the manufacturer's total costs, over that of average total cost, in the form of a taxpayer's subsidy. Under such a plan, the manufacturer or entrepreneur would utilize his managerial skills on behalf of the intellectually underprivileged, and the community would do its part in the form of supporting a federal, state, county or municipal expenditure on behalf of goods produced largely by groups of limited ability.

Such a proposal would lead to a hue and cry from manufacturers. They would label the encouragement of such a plan "unfair competition," with the government showing economic favoritism towards mechanized production as against automated production. In addition, the government would be ridiculed for subsidizing inefficient labor. The former charge would have an element of truth in it. The latter would not. A technologically less efficient process is not the same thing as less efficient human labor. Within the limitations of the fact that production would be accomplished by marginal types of skills, we might conceivably find that the intellectually underprivileged display these skills as well as (and occasionally even better than) average workers.

The American community has to make a choice. Shall we ignore the right to life, liberty and the pursuit of happiness of 25 per cent of our potential labor force? Or shall we ignore a smaller total revenue and net profit for the typical producer in the normal market? We do not hesitate to use the taxpayer's dollar for the production of military hardware or for the advancement of space technology. Why should we hesitate to use it on behalf of that 25 per cent of our population who are temporarily shut out of the labor market through no fault of their own? This is part of what

we mean by a feasible plan which departs radically from conventional thinking but which seeks to confer economic opportunity and a sense of dignity and self-esteem upon the intellectually underprivileged.

In a way, the subsidizing of economic opportunity for the intellectually underprivileged is but another instance of *Parkinson's Law*, which stresses the degree to which human effort is wasted in industrial organization. In Parkinson's words, "Work expands so as to fill the time available for its completion." We fall back on Parkinson's Law, under the plan I have proposed. In the last analysis, the *modern economy* does not need the low-grade services of the intellectually underprivileged. In effect, the plan suggested asks for *part of* the manufacturing sector of the economy to allow itself to become in part labor-intensive, while the rest of the manufacturing sector is cybernating the human factor out of participation.

But is the tendency to fall back on Parkinson's Law such a heinous sin? We make use of Parkinson's Law every day in industry, but almost always on behalf of average or better than average people. The amount of unnecessary paperwork in white-collar occupations is enormous, both in government and industry. We are disinclined to trim away the fat because of humane or political considerations. Industry often accepts the increased costs produced by superfluous labor—or what amounts to the same thing, reduced profits—as an institutional investment in goodwill. Only a *severe threat* to one's profit position will result in a reduction that finally trims off the fat. By the same token, there is every reason in the world to demonstrate the same institutional goodwill towards the intellectually underprivileged. Gabor [11] has actually recognized the social utility of Parkinson's Law in a world that rarely tries to foresee the consequences of new technology, a world still mesmerized by the Puritan ethic of work.

Subsidy of employment for the intellectually underprivileged can be effected under two different types of institutional arrangement. One would be conventional. Intellectually underprivileged employees could be interspersed among average workers in factories located in the existing factory districts of manufacturing communities. Production could be managed by the same kinds of managerial elite with which we are now familiar. The production process, however, would involve a mechanized return to extremely specialized but intellectually undemanding skills, and would not, therefore, resemble production in an up-to-date factory. These would be competitive with the mechanized ones and would be located elsewhere. The second manner in which mechanization could be used to subsidize work for the intellectually underprivileged would be to build special industrial communities in which *all* factory production (regardless of the product-line turned out) was mechanized and intellectually untaxing. The role of management would be the same for these factory units as in the preceding case.

The advantage of industrial, community sites is this: if economic or market conditions, or seasonality, created the need for a reduction in working personnel in one type of factory and an increase of working personnel in another, such transfers could be easily effected. In effect, such specialized industrial communities would possess a permanent flying squadron of operatives who could be shifted easily from one factory unit to another, cutting various kinds of labor costs considerably. Training for new tasks would be of short duration. A sense of personal worth would come from the diversification of relatively simple tasks.

This diversification, which would be part of the labor repertoire of the intellectually underprivileged as a result of frequent transfers, would be extremely worthwhile, psychologically speaking.

Marginal Skills for Underdeveloped Economies

The federal government can try to make the simple skills of the intellectually underprivileged available where they are greatly needed, namely, in some of the underdeveloped countries of the world. Many of these countries are faced with a labor surplus which is relatively inefficient for the preparation of the infra-structure (social capital in the form of roads, dams, energy sources, dwellings and simple types of capital goods) needed for their economies. Adults in these countries, unfamiliar with the unskilled, semiskilled and moderately skilled occupational repertoires of the West, could be trained in such skills. These are precisely those skills that, if available, could accelerate the preparation of the infra-structure. If the U.S. Government were willing to organize labor cadres with marginal skills, send them abroad both to train the unsophisticated, potential labor supply of these countries and to work in them for extended periods and to work out arrangements for payment of salaries, the possibility of an extensive use of the simple skills of the intellectually underprivileged would open up. At the same time, a sense of social and personal worth and of being genuinely needed would develop in such a group.

Decisions must be made as to how such an operation is to be funded and what repayments are to be made to the government by those who go abroad. It would be no insuperable task to work this out. The important thing to remember is the double-edged benefit which results from such an

11

operation. This consists of the encouragement we can give to the rising expectations of prospective friends abroad while, at the same time, providing an opportunity for self-support for the marginally skilled.

Completing the Tasks of Conservation

The establishment at this time of a revived Civilian Conservation Corps could probably create many jobs in which the marginal services of the intellectually underprivileged might be valuably exploited. Many tasks need to be done in connection with conservation, reclamation, reforestation, flood control, irrigation, the elimination of water pollution, the preservation of the natural landscape, gardening, the construction of civic greenhouses, the care of rapidly disappearing game and so on. Many representatives of the population in the I.Q. range 70 to 89 can acquire the skills necessary for the fulfillment of these tasks. The immensity of these tasks can be gathered from a reading of Carson,[12] Udall,[13] Lyons [14] or Cubbedge,[15] to name just a few who have written on such problems. The intellectually underprivileged can be given an opportunity to earn a living by creating social value and, at the same time, they can acquire an unmistakable sense of national mission and personal worth. These latter feelings are certain to be generated as the recognition which such a program merits is given publicity *via* our mass media of communication.

Opening Up the Public Sector of the Economy

Galbraith [16] and many other American economists have argued that we need an extension of public and social services. Many public and social services are inappropriate for the private sector of the economy. The neglect of such services distorts somewhat the pattern of service consumption and fails to produce a social balance between services which stem from the public and the private sources in the economy. Public services which are currently in short supply would, according to Galbraith and others, involve the following objectives: the rebuilding of American cities; the construction of highways, hospitals, schools and airports; the creation of municipal cultural facilities like concert halls, museums, art galleries, neighborhood libraries and publicly owned research institutes; the provision of recreational facilities such as sports fields and stadia, public parks and similar leisure-time outlets; and an attack on municipal problems like air and water pollution.

Now the point underlying our emphasis on the need for more extended public services is this: many of the marginal skills of the intellectually underprivileged can clearly and profitably be used in the fulfillment of these tasks. Many of the occupations and services involved in these tasks are well within the capacities of the intellectually underprivileged. This claim will be easily substantiated by a reading of Super's volume [17] on vocational fitness. Americans must be willing to employ a mixture of relatively inefficient labor from this group and the highly skilled labor associated with the new technology. If all the public services now needed to achieve social balance were given expression through a new type of Works Progress Administration and a new type of Public Works Program, the marginal skills of the intellectually underprivileged would be needed for a long time, perhaps indefinitely.

The taxpayer would, of course, have to be willing to foot the bill. He grumbled, but he assumed it in The Great Depression. In 1933, the worst year, there were never more than 15 to 17 million of working age unemployed. If the modern trend towards cybernation (which eliminates the demand for marginal services) is coupled with the fact that there are 34 million of the intellectually underprivileged potentially in the labor force, then we can clearly foresee the day when the number of the unemployed of working age from this group alone would exceed the depression figure. The latter, it is to be remembered, represented *all levels of ability* in the population. It would therefore make sense for the taxpayer to consent to a burden of increased public services. This would not only provide a future for a fair fraction of his fellow citizens; it would also give the nation something for its money. The public services we need and the social balance we must strive for would not, in any sense, constitute national busywork. They are, instead, *national service lags,* and the lead-time which has already developed from our neglect to provide them should not be allowed to increase. Thus our assumption of these social responsibilities could provide employment for millions of marginal workers, while integrating them more fully into the life of the community. They would not have to be "outsiders" any longer.

Re-establishing Consumer Interest in Handicraft Production

If a successful campaign can be aimed at increasing the consumer's interest in purchasing custom-made goods (such as apparel or hand-made arts and crafts items), the economic opportunities available to the intellectually underprivileged will increase substantially. Institutional purchasing of custom-made items and commodities would considerably aid a shift of this sort. The advantages in durability, individualized design and aesthetic appearance can always be brought to the attention of the American consumer. To be sure, the cultivation of a taste for custom-made goods may be offset by the increase in cost. This was the telling factor in the past, when limited salaries could be made to stretch further by purchasing mass-produced goods (always cheaper than custom-made items produced for the same purpose). Now, however, with the great increase in disposable income, the consumer is less likely to try to balance lowered cost against improved quality. A nationally well-organized and continued campaign for the return of individualized, custom-made commodities, accompanied by color displays in our mass media, State Fairs and commerical exhibits set up for the special purpose of acquainting the average consumer with the advantages of custom-built products, is likely to achieve a measure of success. Practically all of the skills involved in producing custom-made goods are within the range of ability of the intellectually underprivileged. Many past studies in applied and industrial psychology are conspicuous testimony to this fact.

In addition to lending themselves to custom-made production, the aptitudes of the intellectually underprivileged can also be used to provide a range of services, some of which are unavailable at present. Thus a whole series of special services for retirees can be instituted, and considering the steady growth of our old-age population, a wide demand for such services is likely to arise. Many of the services [18] now provided by the government can be shouldered by marginal workers. Hopefully this will be followed either by a tax reduction or, better still, the allocation of federal funds now dispensed for such services to state and municipal agencies, to pay for their *private* provision. Many housing and community services, auxiliary health services and leisure-time services sought by older citizens, such as are described by Burgess,[19] are also well within the capabilities of the intellectually underprivileged. The services supplied to inmates in homes for the aged—institutions which are now rapidly on the increase—can also be dispensed by the minimally skilled.

Finally, we should not overlook an extension of *traditional* services for the average consumer which are well within the range of abilities of marginal workers. Among such services, for instance, are gardening, landscaping, home repair services under the watchful eye of overseers, to nurseries and playgrounds, and the like. A special type of service that the intellectually underprivileged can provide lies along the lines of entertainment. Forming youth orchestras, neighborhood baseball teams, exhibits of arts and crafts, dramatic groups, and so on, interspersing the intellectually underprivileged among individuals of average ability *in groups all of whose members possess the special talents required,* and having the community encourage such services by paying for them, may provide still further economic opportunities for this limited-ability group.

Tomorrow's Technology and the End of Economic Deprivation for All

There is another measure that might solve the economic problem for many people who are scattered over all ranges of ability and educational background. This represents so radical an economic and social innovation that it will meet with great resistance. My only reason for mentioning it here is that it can appropriately be applied rather early in the game to the intellectually underprivileged, should it ever be adopted.

Theobald,[20] convinced that cybernation will gradually eliminate most jobs over the next few decades, has begun to work on economic measures which will provide purchasing power for the unemployed in a society in which human labor will, presumably, no longer be necessary. To convey the flavor of the considerations that have convinced Theobald that work is due to disappear in the United States, let me quote here the views of Bellman,[21] a computer scientist of the Rand Corporation. Theobald [20] has also given considerable thought to Bellman's assertions.

"Industrial automation has reached the point of no return: the pace will increase astronomically in the next decade.

The scientific knowhow to automate American industry almost completely is already available and is certain to be used.

Banks could cut their staffs in half easily by further automation; the steel and automotive industries could increase their use of automation a hundredfold.

Lower and middle management as well as production workers will be displaced, for there will no longer be a need for decision making at that level.

Unemployment resulting from automation would be greater right now except that many industries are holding back—at a sacrifice to their profits . . . to avoid increasing the severity of the problem. 'Self restraint on the part of industries cannot continue indefinitely.'

Automation itself will produce few jobs.

Two per cent of the population—by implication the 2 per cent at the upper administrative and executive levels—will, in the discernible future, be able to produce all the goods and services needed to feed, clothe and run our society with the aid of machines."

To guarantee purchasing power for all, Theobald [20] proposes to distribute money *not based upon work done*—money which will be essentially a credit claim on the gross national product. Without discussing the rationale of Theobald's plans, let us only mention here that individuals would receive either a "Basic Economic Security Payment," in the neighborhood of $3,200 per family, or a sum known as "Committed Spending," in the neighborhood of $10,000.

On the assumption that such a plan—or one like it—may be welcomed in the future, it is easy to see that, under its beneficence, the intellectually underprivileged will at least be able to find a consumption-niche for themselves. Under Theobald's proposals, "Committed Spending" is intended to bulwark the middle-income group in this country. It is therefore highly probable that individuals of limited ability and marginal skills, who have in fact never had an opportunity to achieve middle-class status, will have to be content with Basic Economic Security Payments.

One can pass no judgment here on the arguments of Theobald or the feasibility of his proposals. What is important in the present context, however, is that if such proposals or proposals similar to them come to pass, they may provide an all-time solution for the intellectually underprivileged.

The Agony of the Present—a Summing Up

We now close our discussion of the problems that have to be faced by the economic orphans of our technologic civilization. These economic orphans are not only industrially illiterate; they are also illiterate in the more usual sense of the term. Their industrial illiteracy is, unfortunately, profoundly related to their general illiteracy. Sylvia Porter, in her syndicated column of April 26, 1965, has this to say:

"There is no doubt that industry is becoming increasingly hostile to any job applicant with less than a high school diploma. Many corporations won't even interview a job seeker unless he is a high school graduate.

The illiterate is at a disadvantage not only because he can't follow instructions for industrial machinery, take telephone messages, add up a bill at a corner grocery store or sign a personal check. He also is often incapable of absorbing training and retraining programs which have become a part of today's industrial life and which are predicated on a knowledge of elementary educational skills."

Miss Porter points out the indirect costs of such illiteracy: physical and mental illness, urban blight, crime, delinquency, illegitimacy and so on. She stresses the intangible costs in terms of individual indignities suffered by the intellectually underprivileged in later life. The industrial scrapheap to which the illiterate is confined represents a waste of human life, our most precious resource. The stark disaster that illiteracy and semi-literacy portend in a technologic civilization is perhaps indicated by the fact that unemployment in urban centers runs to about 50 per cent among the totally illiterate and about 25 per cent among the semi-literate. A recent Chicago study showed that nearly two-thirds of those on welfare rolls had less than a sixth grade education.

The economic impact of illiteracy on the American economy as a whole has been estimated by Dr. Edward W. Brice, chief of adult education of the Office of Education in Washington. The economic "drag" caused by illiteracy and undereducation—the difference between what illiterates and semiliterates earn and what they *could* earn with a minimum of *basic* education—has been estimated to be 100 billion dollars. This is the equivalent of almost one-sixth of the current gross national product.*

One has to emphasize that, although not all illiterates are among the intellectually underprivileged, many and perhaps most of the intellectually underprivileged are among the total illiterates and the semiliterates of a technologic civilization. We

---

* The gross national product for 1964 was officially 622.6 billions of dollars.

know that there are 37.2 million American adults in the United States who have had less than a grade school education. If to these we add the intellectually underprivileged who have had some secondary school training or who have managed to complete a high school education on the basis of either low local standards or social promotions, the number of illiterates and semi-literates (this latter classification being, probably, the more accurate category in which to classify many of the intellectually underprivileged) would clearly reach an appallingly higher figure. Miss Porter's facts and warnings, therefore, deserve mature and intelligent attention. A technologic and competitive civilization that neglects the economic needs of the intellectually underprivileged is courting disaster.

We have tried, in this paper, to describe the economic and occupational dilemmas of the intellectually underprivileged—those in the I.Q. range 70 to 89—in a world growing increasingly complex. We have also tried to suggest means by which the intellectually underprivileged can be provided with economic opportunities to achieve a self-supporting status, in spite of the fact that their skills and services tend to be industrially marginal. There is no pretense here that these are the only proposals which can be made, or even that they are the best ones. The objective of the present paper is more modest: to emphasize the economic and occupational problems faced by those who are intellectually marginal in a modern, complex society. This is the group that—when all is said and done —occupies an economic no-man's-land between the custodial needs of the mentally deficient and the great mass of the average citizenry, who can be counted upon to be self-supporting. Inasmuch as they are too capable to be considered for custodial care and too ineffective to support themselves,

they are in an economic hell. Therefore, the solution to the dilemma in which they find themselves must now be recognized as a long-term community responsibility.

REFERENCES

1. Buber, Martin, I and Thou. New York, Scribner's, 1958.

2. Penrose, Lionel S., The Biology of Mental Defect. New York, Grune and Stratton, 1949. See Chapter VI, "The Genetics of Intelligence."

3. Kallman, Franz Josef, Heredity in Health and Mental Disorder. New York, Norton, 1953. See Chapter IV, "Convulsive Disease, Gene-controlled Neurologic Disorders, and Various Types of Mental Defect," particularly Section C, entitled "Mental Deficiency."

4. See Cattell, Raymond B., Personality: A Systematic Theoretical and Factual Study. New York, McGraw-Hill, 1950; Personality and Motivation: Structure and Measurement. Yonkers, New York, World Books, 1957.

5. Hogben, Lancelot, Nature and Nurture. London, Allen and Unwin, 1945. See Chapter V, "The Interdependence of Nature and Nurture," and Appendix III.

6. Rostand, Jean, Can Man Be Modified? New York, Basic Books, 1959.

7. Carrel, Alexis, Man, The Unkown. West Drayton, Middlesex, England, Penguin Books, 1948.

8. Missenard, André, In Search of Man. New York, Hawthorn Books, 1957.

9. du Noüy, Lecomte, Human Destiny. New York, Signet Books, 1947.

10. Simpson, George Gaylord, The Meaning Of Evolution. New York, Mentor Books, 1951.

11. Gabor, Dennis, Inventing The Future. London, Secker and Warburg, 1963.

12. Carson, Rachel, Silent Spring. Boston, Houghton Mifflin, 1962.

13. Udall, Stewart L., The Quiet Crisis. New York, Avon Books, 1963.

14. Lyons, Barrow, Tomorrow's Birthright: A Political and Economic Interpretation of Our Natural Resources. New York, Funk and Wagnalls, 1955.

15. Cubbedge, Robert E., The Destroyers of America. New York, Macfadden Books, 1964.

16. Galbraith, John Kenneth, The Affluent Society. Boston, Houghton Mifflin, 1958.

17. Super, Donald E., Appraising Vocational Fitness. New York, Harper, 1949.

18. Report to the President: How the Government Works for Older People. Washington, D.C., Federal Council on Aging, 1962.

19. Burgess, Ernest W., Aging In Western Societies. Chicago, University Of Chicago Press, 1960.

20. Theobald, Robert, Free Men and Free Markets. New York, Clarkson N. Potter, 1963.

21. Quoted by Robert Theobald, The Educational Record, 45:113 (Spring 1964).

CYBERNATION:

Its Implications for
Culture and Education

The Cybernation Revolution has been defined as the industrial and economic breakthrough which has been brought about by the combination of the computer and the automated self-regulating machine. The signers of the document which has come to be known as The Manifesto Of The Ad Hoc Committee On The Triple Revolution,[1] have seen in cybernation[2] an augur of a new society which will possess a system of almost unlimited productive capacity and one which will require less and less human toil as time goes on. These signers — and others who have been subsequently impressed by the arguments of the Manifesto — foresee eventually a workless world and hope that the leisure potentially capable of being created for all will result in a High Culture the like of which presumably has never before been recorded in human history. The achievement of High Culture, however, in a cybernating society presents problems which many who are enthusiastic over the promise of cybernation have ignored almost completely. I should like to discuss two of these problems here. One of these has to do with the relation of cybernation and leisure to the social complexity of a dawning new age. The other has to do with the contrast between the educational needs of a cybernating society and its inescapable legacy of contemporary Mass Culture.

THE MARRIAGE OF TECHNOCRACY AND MERITOCRACY.[3] High Culture is generally defined in terms of perceptiveness to ideas in science, philosophy and religion, together with a cultivated sensitivity to various types of moral and aesthetic experience. There is a way, however, of organizing

CIMARRON REVIEW, 1969, vol. 8, 42-52.

human experience so as to define High Culture in a more perceptive fashion. Leisure or *the perceptive use of free time* moves in a direction aimed at satisfying seven archetypal relationships. These are man's relationship to himself, to his fellow man, to the opposite sex, to work, to society, to Nature and to what existentialist philosophers call *The Mystery Of Being*. When these relationships are satisfied perceptively men succeed in achieving self-realization, in expanding the horizons of consciousness and creativity, and in increasing the possibilities for self-transcendence in the human community. When these seven fundamental archetypal relationships *are not satisfied* men are then immersed in a variety of tragic forms of alienation. The desire to achieve satisfying relationships of this type is basically the perennial Utopian vision which has moved men since recorded history began.

Karl Mannheim[4] has given us a moving description of the brutishness and ennui that would persist for a human condition which lacked a Utopian vision which, in connection with various possibilities for social order, he referred to as "the morphological perspective." A cybernating society must possess this morphological perspective if science and technology are to be its allies rather than its enemies. A cybernating society can respect the cogency of Ellul's[5] pessimistic analysis of the trends in modern industrialism while rejecting his conviction that the technological society cannot be deployed for moral ends, that is, for any Utopian vision which would limit the unmanaged growth of technology itself. If Ellul's pessimism were sound then amelioristic planning, which takes the long view on the social effects of cybernation, would be a waste of time. The management of social change producible by science and technology is clearly intended to realize a preset budget of humane social, moral, and cultural purposes.

President Johnson's Great Society, although well intentioned, is the epitome of organization for prosperity, for vocational and status-seeking education and for what has been called a "fun morality." A fun morality uses free time predominantly for purposes of *rest, relaxation and recreation*. It does not seek *renewal* or *developmental leisure* in the intellectual and spiritual sense sought by High Culture. Renewal, in this sense, provides for types of personal and social change which result in an improvement of the seven archetypal relationships to which I have already referred. The obsessive quest for rest, relaxation and recreation is precisely the earmark of Mass Culture. In a general sense no aspects of Mass Culture seek to express satisfactory forms of the seven archetypal relationships already mentioned. In this sense true leisure is the pursuit of High Culture in these forms, and Mass Culture is the expression of any activity which — no matter how distracting, diverting or pleasant — does not take the improvement of these archetypal relationships as its direct objective.

A cybernating society must recognize that it must fulfill these moral imperatives of High Culture. It must recognize at the same time that its heritage from the present will be a Mass Culture whose spirit is intractable to such high purposes. This intractability stems in large part from the almost complete loss in our time of the Utopian vision. It was the content of this vision, which, in the past, moved the partisans of both democracy and socialism. Writers like the historian, H. Stuart Hughes,[6] and the Rhodes Scholar, Kenneth Kenniston,[7] who draws upon a background in both philosophy and psychology, have both emphasized the current loss of what Mannheim called the morphological perspective and which was the real content of democracy. The ideology of democracy has now been transformed into a vision of rampant materialism — a come-and-get-it outlook on life — accompanied by a philosophical negativism which rests on weariness, on apathy and on a passive acceptance of whatever is done by decision-makers. Today even professors — not to be confused with intellectuals — can be found huddled together in their caps and gowns, singing "Che sera, sera." Our entire society is infested with a virus which promotes a tacit agreement not to discuss potentially divisive issues. Hughes — referring to our contemporary loss of Utopian vision — expresses the situation most succinctly in the following fashion:

> . . . I believe we have lost that vision: most of us are quite satisfied with the ugliness of our cities, the waste in our economy, the cheerful incompetence of our leaders, the meaninglessness of public discourse, the general insensibility to the overwhelming danger that threatens us. Along with our vision, we have lost our capacity for indignation, our ability to feel a cosmic anger with what we see going on around us. And until we regain this vision, these capacities, our culture will continue to be what it is today — "weary, flat, stale, and unprofitable." (p. 147)

The opposite of High Culture is, of course, Mass Culture, and the themes of Mass Culture are the most expressive contemporary forms of our loss of the Utopian vision. A cybernating society, most of whose population will be the beneficiaries of Mass Culture in its present forms, will have its hands full in trying to persuade its citizens to use their free time wisely. The prospective leadership of a cybernating society has to be reminded that more free time will not necessarily result in the pursuit of High Culture. The latter conveys the proper sense of the term, *leisure*. There is every reason in the world to expect that the increased free time of a cybernating society will be used chiefly for rest, relaxation and recreation. In support of such pessimism let us tear a leaf from history. From about the middle of the first century AD to Hadrian's reign (117-138), the "height" of the Empire, Rome enjoyed at least one day of holi-

20

day for every working day.[8] Thus freedom from toil was available for at least 50 per cent of the populace's waking time.

This non-cybernated society which had so much free time also possessed a Mass Culture of its own — different from ours in the activities pursued but identical with ours in that these activities were also almost excusively preoccupied with recreation. And what were these pursuits as reported by the great writers of antiquity? The Roman plebs seemed to be chiefly concerned with food, fun and fornication, and plain honesty forces me to recognize that at least two of these three terms are redundant. Spelled out, this meant that the masses were interested in barbaric public games, organized on a colossal scale, which included gladiatorial shows, wild-beast fights, chariot-racing and theatrical shows. To these games were added the pleasures of the table and the public cultivation of gluttony, so revoltingly characteristic of the freedman, Trimalchio, and his associates, as described by Petronius.[9] Commonplace even in the middle of the Roman social structure were the extravagances of men with money — extravagances which were not limited to the imperial court. Veblen[10] would have called this conspicuous consumption. Capping all of this — although more marked in later Roman times — was the lupanar, the brothel sanctified by Church and State, presumably to protect women of virtuous character but actually to keep men's hormones from popping too violently. It was noticed more than once, however, that the excuse of protecting female virtue did not prevent certain virtuous ladies of leisure from volunteering their services to lupanars frequented by scholars and students. These ladies, it might be said, were Roman female culture-hounds who were always on the prowl, looking for an intellectual who was not so ineffectual when it came to being sexual.

All the above is not a pretty picture. It was, however, the Mass Culture of a society which once had more free time than Western, technological societies have today. It should be clear that its range of popular taste and activity was successfully pursued without benefit of Fortran, Cobol or Algol, although these faithful *linguae francae* of the modern computer may yet indirectly provide the masses of a cybernating society with more time for orgiastic frenzies. Current forms of Mass Culture are not too far removed from the Roman lowbrow's idea of gracious living. The greater amounts of free time promised by a cybernating society — if used to widen the range of activities now so characteristic of Mass Culture — are not a prospect to excite the mind. Nor is it a prospect to move the spirit of the thoughtful, the sensitive and the socially altruistic.

Writers like Gilbert Seldes[11] and Edward Shils[12] see in the various forms of Mass Culture to which our citizenry devotes its leisure, phenomena which they feel are pregnant with social meaning. I have tried long and hard to see what these writers are driving at. If contemporary forms of Mass Culture are, indeed, pregnant with meaning, then all I can say is that the only way to get at that meaning seems to require a Caesarean operation — at least in an intellectual sense. Mass Culture *does not* provide the promise of a satisfactory fulfillment of the archetypal relationships of which I have already spoken.

Let us now consider one of the problems raised by the contrast of High Culture with Mass Culture, precisely because these contrasts are likely to be aggravated under the aegis of a cybernating society. I am referring here to the painful and undeniable trend for the modern advance of knowledge to create two intellectually contrasting subcultures in our midst. Hermann Hesse[13] in his Nobel Prize winning novel, *Magister Ludi* (The Bead Game), has described a community whose intellectual leadership has attempted to reduce all knowledge to a single principle expressed in the form of a mathematically and symbolically universal language of the intellect. Gradually the Magister Ludi or High Priest of the Game comes to realize that the community's desire to see life strictly in cognitive terms, is not very satisfying. Furthermore, and more importantly, he becomes convinced that the true task of the intellectual is to maintain contact with the common man — a completely unrealizable objective in a world in which communication is dominated by intellectual abstractions of a very high order.

The activities of this community inescapably result in the alienation of its members from the average citizen and the preoccupation of the average citizen with cultural activities which Russell Lynes[14] would call "middlebrow" and which serve no socially useful purpose in the world described by Hesse. To make matters worse the average citizen of that world could neither comprehend it nor participate in its direction. It was a world he never made. Critics have seen in Hesse's work a symbolic warning of what lies in store for a society whose decision-making is dominated exclusively by technique, in which mathematics, logic and the thoughtways of science determine the sole forms of communication and become the leading means for determining social change. Such a society must inevitably become bimodal, consisting of a dominant but small and intellectual super-elite and a great mass of ordinary men and women who must seek their intellectual satisfactions elsewhere. More modern forms of this concern over the coming intellectual dichotomy within our social order have been exhibited by Donald Michael[15] and John Wilkinson.[16]

Michael[17] has stressed his conviction that in a cybernating society the research realm of scientists, the problems of government, and the interplay between these two will lie beyond the ken of even our college graduates, so that *a fortiori* one can suppose these matters will be utterly and intellectually alien to the common man. As Michael sees it specialists in computing-machine technology and various types of cyberneticians will be responsible for social, scientific and technological decisions creating social change, whose *raison d'être* cannot effectively be communicated to the average man. In this same vein John Wilkinson, on the staff of the Center for the Study of Democratic Institutions, and translator of Ellul's highly significant analysis of modern life in a volume entitled *The Technological Society,* has raised similar considerations. In a brochure entitled *The Quantitative Society or, What Are You To Do With Noodle?* Wilkinson has dealt with the place of Noodles in a cybernating society. Noodles constitute the great bloc of average men and women in the American middle class — the sellers of real estate or insurance and, in general, the workers in the upper reaches of the white-collar paradise and the lower levels of subprofessional and managerial occupations. Wilkinson, like Michael, is also pessimistic about Noodle's capacity to understand our increasing social complexity, and he puts it this way:

> The contention that persons ignorant of technology can function
> in a democracy to any effect when the society is a technological
> one is dubious. Understanding is not only a prerequisite of control, it *is* control . . . (p. 23)

All the preceding then represents one leisure-time dilemma of American society, both as it exists now and in the immediate future. The values of leisure as renewal and the emphasis on developmental leisure are alien to mass culture in America. The difficulties are aggravated by the fact that the lower quarter of the distribution of human intelligence is probably separated from the values of developmental leisure because these demand aptitudes which are not part of the natural gifts of the poorly endowed. Will a cybernated society then be facing a civilization of two cultures — the culture of the alpha-moron, on the one hand, and the epsilon-normal and beta-bright, on the other? Will a cybercultural society controlled, as it inevitably must be, by the beta-bright, even permit the continuation of a mass culture for the alpha-moron? How will the epsilon-normals and the beta-brights of a cybernated society protect themselves against the smoldering and destructive resentment of a psychological proletariat disfranchised from participation in a world they never made? Must the historian of the future be prepared to describe a new age of revolution known as *The Revolt Of The Low IQ's?*

Nor are dangers absent for those in the middle range of intelligence, the epsilon-normals. We shall probably have to learn how to inculcate a taste in the average man for ideas and theories of the type characteristically provided by science, mathematics, philosophy, etc. Does all this mean then that the beta-brights will be left alone to pursue their cybernated outlooks, come hell and high water? I think not. The outlook of the technician in an Age of Cyberculture will have to be tempered by an education which promotes the fusion of facts and values, in precisely the sense advocated recently by Maslow.[18] The cybernetician and technician of the future will have to make humane values part of the warp and woof of his own inner being rather than dealing with them as mere verbal abstractions. The needed revamping of modern education is long overdue in this respect. When it comes it will have to be concerned with those matters best expressed in the following words of Maslow:

> The final and unavoidable conclusion is that education — like all our social institutions — must be concerned with its final values, and this in turn is just about the same as speaking of what have been called "spiritual values" or "higher values." These are the principles of choice which help us to answer the age-old "spiritual" (philosophical? religious? humanistic? ethical?) questions: What is the good life? What is the good man? The good woman? What is the good society and what is my relation to it? What are my obligations to society? What is best for my children? What is justice? Truth? Virtue? What is my relation to nature, to death, to aging, to pain, to illness? How can I live a zestful, enjoyable, meaningful life? What is my responsibility to my brothers? Who *are* my brothers? What shall I be loyal to? What must I be ready to die for? (p. 52)

When, and only when, the educational matters referred to above have been properly dealt with, will leisure come into its own. Until then, the use of leisure-time will continue to be a fundamental problem for Americans — spiritually, intellectually and culturally.

EDUCATION IN THE CYBERNATING SOCIETY VERSUS COMMUNICATION IN MASS CULTURE. The cybernating society will inherit two aspects of Mass Culture which augur ill for its future. I am referring to *homogenization* and *kitsch*. Because these two aspects of mass culture contravene the possibility of using leisure time for renewal and because they are so germane to certain major technological developments which presage a new world-a-coming, so far as leisure is concerned, they must be separately treated.

Homogenization, as applied to, say, the content of a popular magazine or a radio news broadcast, refers to the failure to discriminate among the values of the different materials brought to the reader's or listener's attention. Thus an issue of a popular magazine will devote an equal number of pages to the following features: famous stars of the stage and screen who have made a comeback from alcoholism; courtship customs in the islands of the Pacific; recent discoveries in nuclear physics which promise to revolutionize our understanding of matter; the political views of retirees who live in Bellyache, North Dakota; and the latest hobbies of teen-agers in Harlem. The significant is lumped with the sensational;

the lasting is coupled with the transient; the noble is married to the debased. The presentation and style tend to imply that everything is just about as important as anything else and that the educational and cultural value of one feature is just about the same as any other. A similar phenomenon occurs during news broadcasts. With no change of tone the announcer will slip from comments on an earthquake and tidal wave which destroyed 20,000 lives in northern Japan to the observation that Stan Musial sprained his leg in the ball park in today's game and may be unable to play for several days. In the same flat and deadpan voice he will remark that during the first six months of this year one million children died of starvation in underdeveloped nations and that a waitress in Hollywood accused Rock Hudson of being the father of her child. About the same amount of time will be given to all news items. It matters not that one news item seems to carry the threat of an uprising and civil war in Bolivia while another suggests only that women's skirts will be an inch shorter this year. Everything has the same momentous significance or the same boring unimportance.

Kitsch is the term we apply to those products of mass culture — via the mass media — in which all the aesthetic work is done for the reader, spectator, or listener. The message is built into, rather than drawn out of, the product. The recipient is told what he is supposed to feel and think. The sweep of symbol and allegory is replaced by the visually concrete image. Intellectual depth is eliminated for an artificial simplicity of problem and confrontation to which social life is nowhere tangent. The consumer of mass culture must never be emotionally taxed or swept up in nuances and conflicts beyond his limited spiritual attention. He must be rendered unaware of complexity. If a classic is to be brought to his attention via stage or screen or via a printed popularization, its meaning must be either explained in a corrupted and distorted fashion or it must be explained away entirely. This, then, is *kitsch*.

Just as there is a *"kitsch"* of high culture and high art, so there is a *"kitsch"* in the life of the mind and the spirit. All the woebegone efforts of experimental education, which hope to create understanding without intellectual strain in the student, without developing habits of intellectual organization and analysis, are *"kitsch"* in this sense. If you have learned to enjoy educational *"kitsch"* you cannot be intellectually serious. You simply do not know what the word "serious" corresponds to in either a psychological or an intellectual sense. Likewise all the efforts to play at culture by providing students with rapid surveys of literature and the arts are equally doomed. This is *"kitsch"* of the spirit which hopes to convey the existentialist content of frustration, suffering, disappointment, human struggle and shattered and renovated ideals, through abstractions rather than through personal experience. None of the passion and power of great art, none of its capacity to probe into the motivational grounds of personal striving and to convey the gap between our real and our alleged motives, can become part of the spiritual warp and woof of any individual for whom life has thus far not created meaningful tensions which have been worked through. Such growth tensions cannot be provided by what we now call "gracious living." Nor can gracious living establish a vital center nor promote the full expression of a personal idiom.

It is such lack of experience that makes it utter folly to expect a boy who has thus far been interested only in baseball batting averages to write Haiku poetry or be sensitive to its intentions, content, or purpose. It is absurdity to the *n*th degree to try to teach economics, science, mathematics or philosophy to youngsters who have no comprehension of the four fundamental operations of arithmetic. The writing of Haiku poetry which is a meaningless chore and the bored submission to principles which are not even minimally grasped are both guaranteed to make the development of seriousness impossible. Yet without such seriousness the use of free time for developmental leisure, that is, for renewal, is completely out of the question. Renewal is maximally achieved through the Greek ideals of *paideia* which stress personal development and the promotion of a sense of civic and social consciousness. Cultivation of the Greek ideals of *paideia* must depend on *"spondaitos"* or appropriate seriousness.

The one time in the average American's life when he *may escape* *"kitsch"* of the spirit and move towards the content of the Greek ideals of *paideia,* is when he is an undergraduate. I am referring particularly to undergraduate ideals of radicalism, evangelism and Bohemianism, as described by Matza,[19] although these ideals rub off soon enough when undergraduates who hold them "go secular." However, their adoption during one's undergraduate days is largely a product of the pressures from certain *undergraduate subcultures* and, in no sense, reflects a deliberate planning by some young people for their own developmental leisure. *"Kitsch"* of the spirit is built into the *intellectual goulash* which we now call the liberal arts tradition and, because of this fact, it is quite fair to say that the liberal arts atmosphere of the modern college or university is not, *in most cases,* conducive to the later appearance of a concern for developmental leisure and, *a fortiori,* a later use of free time actually devoted to the pursuit of such leisure.

Other American institutions contribute to the intellectual and spiritual superficiality of the times. Book-of-the-Month Clubs and amateur theatricals (in which the playwright is never understood and the emotions with which he is so deeply concerned are run through by stage-struck lasses with neuro-muscular gifts but little empathy) will also pro-

26

vide the possibility for playing at culture without being serious. Further cases in point are the playing at culture by "listening to good music" and "looking at great paintings" while never becoming involved with the materials, theme, mood, and message, as did the composer or the artist. Popular books on science which humanely pretend to help the reader to understand very difficult matters without any effort greater than that required to discriminate between two diagrams or pictures also help to provide the shadow as a substitute for the substance and leave the reader unable to see the intellectual forest of science for the factual trees so gratuitously provided by the author. At the same time the spirit of the intellectually disciplinary methods of science is never caught at all. It would not be difficult to provide a bill of particulars showing many other current popular activities which aid and abet the decline of seriousness.

I have taken pains to emphasize the outstanding roles played by homogenization and kitsch in mass culture because, as I have already remarked they are both phenomena which contravene the possibility of using leisure time for renewal. They reflect the kind of stimulation which mass man has come to expect from mass culture, and they determine the nature of the activities which he is likely to pursue in his free time. The leisure-time dilemma of American culture and civilization lies in the fact that, under the impact of science and technology, we are rapidly moving towards a civilization in which leisure may increase rather rapidly and substantially. Were this to happen we would be faced with more time for more people. The question which would .then naturally arise is whether this substantial increment of time is to be devoted to more mass culture which promotes homogenization and kitsch or more free time for developmental leisure in the sense of renewal. The former would give us a civilization which would be an air-conditioned nightmare. The latter would give us a civilization which would move rapidly towards the fulfillment of the Greek ideals of personal development and social responsibility, together with the promise of fulfillment of all the millenial dreams which have moved men in their quest for the good life.

REFERENCES

1. The complete text of The Manifesto will be found, together with commentary on it in *Liberation*, April 1964, pp. 9-15.
2. This term was introduced by Donald Michael in the following work: Donald Michael. *Cybernation: The Silent Conquest*. Santa Barbara, California. Center For The Study Of Democratic Institutions, 1962, 48 pp.
3. Michael Young, the British sociologist, coined the term *meritocracy* to describe the dangers and absurdities of a social structure which insists that only high IQ's may rise to the top and become our decision-makers. See Michael Young.

The Rise of the Meritocracy, 1870-2033. An Essay on Education and Equality. Harmondsworth, Middlesex, England: Penguin Books, 1963. 190 pp.

4. Karl Mannheim. *Ideology and Utopia*. An Introduction to the Sociology of Knowledge. New York: Harcourt, Brace, 1936. 318 pp.

5. Jacques Ellul. *The Technological Society*. New York: Alfred A. Knopf, 1964. 449 pp.

6. H. Stuart Hughes. *An Essay for Our Times*. New York: Alfred A. Knopf, 1951. 196 pp.

7. Kenneth Kenniston. "Alienation and the Decline of Utopia." pp 79-117. In *Varieties of Modern Social Theory* (Hendrik M. Ruitenbeck, ed.) New York: E. P. Dutton, 1963. 434 pp.

8. See Jerome Carcopino. *Daily Life in Ancient Rome*. New Haven, Connecticut: Yale University Press, 1940. 342 pp.

9. Petronius, Nero's friend, left us a picture of the extravagance, vulgarity, and gluttony of a Roman banquet in the *Satirica* — a banquet which was given by the vulgar millionaire, Trimalchio. Gilbert Highet has, however, questioned the authenticity of Petronius' picture for the wealthy in Rome, maintaining that the vulgar superstitions and ostentations which Petronius described were characteristic of Levantine freedmen and not of true Romans.

10. Thorstein Veblen. *The Theory of the Leisure Class*. An Economic Study of Institutions. New York: Mentor Books, 1953. 261 pp.

11. Gilbert Seldes. *The Seven Lively Arts*. New York: Harper & Brothers, 1924. 398 pp.

12. Edward Shils. "Mass Society and Its Culture." pp. 1-27. In *Culture for the Millions?* (Norman Jacobs, ed.) Princeton, New Jersey: D. Van Nostrand, 1959. 200 pp.

13. Hermann Hesse. *Magister Ludi (The Bead Game)*. New York: Frederick Ungar Publishing Company, 1964. 502 pp.

14. Russel Lynes. "Highbrow, Lowbrow, Middlebrow." pp. 310-333. In *The Tastemakers*. New York: Harper & Brothers, 1954. 362 pp.

15. *Op. cit.*

16. John Wilkinson. *The Quantitative Society or, What Are You to do with Noodle?* Santa Barbara, California: Center for the Study of Democratic Institutions, 1964. 32 pp.

17. *Op. cit.* For an easily understood and fairly complete picture of some of the social changes which lie ahead, as a result of cybernation, the reader may wish to consult the following recent volume: Donald Michael. *The Next Generation*. The Prospects Ahead for the Youth of Today and Tomorrow. New York: Random House, 1965. 218 pp.

18. Abraham Maslow. *Religions, Values, and Peak-Experiences*. Columbus, Ohio: Ohio State University Press, 1964. 123 pp.

19. David Matza. "Subterranean Traditions of Youth." *The Annals of the American Academy of Political and Social Science. Teen Age Culture*. Vol. 338 (November 1961) 102-118. (Jessie Bernard, Special Editor).

two proposed new institutions for the creation of world union

1. The Need For New Institutions Of International Goodwill

The need for the promotion of international goodwill and increased international understanding of the global problems of our age and the need for a new kind of education on the issues which rack nations, groups and individuals and which will provide a more widespread dissemination of the available, alternative solutions for meeting these problems and issues, are more pressing than ever before. Just as important is the need to reduce or eliminate twentieth century parochialism—the product largely of political propaganda—and this means the use of new types of institutions which will acquaint large numbers of people with an accurate idea of how other peoples live. However, these desiderata cannot be best met in terms of traditional procedures and familiar institutions. Many new types of social invention, of international institution and of unfamiliar procedures are needed to meet these needs. The attempt to requite them with outworn methods and habits of thought tends not only to be futile, with little pay-off, but also tends to reach rather limited audiences and usually audiences of a specialized nature. What is most needed at the present time are institutional and social inventions which, *in principle*, can reach a mass audience or, at least, a large public of citizens who are not specialists on international issues and other ways of life. If citizens of intelligence and goodwill are willing to be educated along lines which will provide increased international understanding and goodwill and if various publics composed of average citizens are willing to acquaint themselves with information and experiences concerning other cultural ways of life, then we can expect that such approaches will be conducive to a friendlier and more sophisticated cosmopolitanism. Under such circumstances the formation of an enlightened but mass public opinion with respect to the characteristics of other peoples as well as the true nature of international issues, will be assured.

There are a considerable number of such innovations available, some of which are being tried and many of which have not as yet been put into practice at all. Thus a nation's ship which moves from country to country supplying medicines and medical services for the sick, certainly increases goodwill for that nation. The use of the Peace Corps adds a dimension to the U.S. image in foreign eyes. Foreign exchange students who live abroad, whether these be at the secondary school or college level, promote greater understanding in their home countries of the countries they visit. But all of these innovations reach rather limited audiences. Cultural exchange programs reach wider audiences but —apart from the fact that these are usually what would be called middle-class audiences in the West—they are too infrequent and too limited in scope to have lasting effects or to generate the understanding of conflicting issues or of other peoples, both of which are so badly needed at the present time. What is more profoundly needed

WORLD UNION, First Quarter, 1968, vol. 8, 15-23.

are social inventions and institutions for these purposes which either can be given a mass base immediately or which are potentially capable of attracting such a base.

Professor Billington[1] of Princeton University, attacking this problem in America's most widely disseminated periodical, *Life*, has this to say in speaking of the conflicts and tensions which exist between the U.S. and U.S.S.R.

"A dramatic acceleration of person-to-person exchanges, bypassing all political and bureaucratic methods of selection, would expose the two peoples to each other in depth for the first time. Among many possibilities are large-scale, preferably extended exchanges between peoples of roughly similar regions: i.e., San Francisco-Vladivostok, Duluth-Petrozavodsk, Texas-the Ukranian Republic, oil fields by the Gulf of Mexico and by the Caspian Sea, etc.

If increased people-to-people contact might help overcome mutual ignorance, the launching of some new binational Russo-American scientific and cultural projects might start us on the path toward new practical forms of collaboration that should help bypass old hostilities. Such projects (preferably under auspices of the U.N.) would never seek to exclude others, and should begin with projects of common concern to all humanity. For instance, a publicly declared binational war on cancer or heart disease would need and invite the participation of others while distracting our own peoples somewhat from current conflicts. These gestures do not, of course, deal directly with the outstanding problems dividing the power elites of the two countries. Fresh initiatives may also be possible at this level—say, in the direction of a joint commitment to convert military into economic development aid in some area of the "third world," where we have in effect been superimposing our own conflicts on others." (p.84)

One should notice that Professor Billington is explicitly calling for mass-based projects or for projects which are potentially capable of having a mass base. When one reads, for instance, the descriptions given by Fanon[2] of the miseries created for colonial peoples, sometimes deliberately and sometimes inadvertently, by the colonial powers, it is easier to recognize that the hatred and frustration which these have induced can be eliminated or reversed only by the development of institutions and procedures which will not only be highly novel but which will be mass based. Anything less than this is essentially a kind of political preciousness and an exercise in futility, serving to expiate the sense of moral guilt among the "favoured of the earth," but hardly conducive to a realistic, large-scale elimination of the abuses described by Fanon.

But it should not be thought that the needed social inventions must be intended chiefly for the wretched of the earth. Even more can be accomplished if the better educated, comfortable but concerned publics of the advanced countries can be made acquainted with other cultures and ways of life, with international issues and with the sources of international conflict. These are the publics whose members are in the best position to register both their convictions and their wishes and thereby, hopefully, influence the course of events. These are also the publics in

[1] James H. Billington. "The Intelligentsia." *Life.* Vol. 63, No. 19, November 10, 1967, 70-84.

[2] Frantz Fanon. *The Wretched Of The Earth.* With a preface by Jean-Paul Sartre. New York: Grove Press, 1966. 255 pp.

which the seeds of international understanding and goodwill will flower best and furnish the greatest spiritual pay-off.

There are a considerable number of new social inventions reducing the parochialism and tensions of our time for the purposes I have mentioned, which I intend to describe in later publications. In the present paper, however, I wish to restrict myself to the description of only two of these, the goodwill enclave and the international newspaper. Without more ado, then, let me proceed with my exposition of these two possibilities.

2. The Goodwill Enclave

If our objective is to contribute to joint cultural understanding between any two countries which are in conflict today—such as the U.S. and the U.S.S.R.—an increase of such joint cultural understanding can be promoted, I believe, by the establishment of a new institution which I propose to christen "the goodwill enclave." This would be essentially the organisation of a *typical* community, such as is to be found in country A and one which will be transplanted into country B. The site to be selected in country B for an enclave of this sort is to be one located in some favourable and pleasant environment. This environment, however, will never be anywhere near a large, urban centre of B. Nevertheless, the enclave will be so located that it will be easily reachable by minor roads to be constructed and which lead from main highways in B to the enclave in question. The *typicality* of the enclave will be reflected in its social life, its cultural activities, its educational pursuits, its use of leisure, its political institutions for self-government, the occupations of its members, its social and group activities, leisure-time pursuits and functions, its family, courtship and marriage customs, its agricultural practices, the dress and customs of its people, etc. In short an enclave of this sort will have to be small—anywhere from

five to fifteen thousand people, which is a smaller population than can be found on some of our larger, American campuses—and will therefore not contain *heavy industry*. Since, however, large-scale technology and management tend to be fairly similar in most advanced countries,[1] this type of institution does not differ very much throughout the world and its absence will, therefore, in no sense lessen the amount of cross-cultural understanding a goodwill enclave can. be expected to promote.

How shall the members of a goodwill enclave be chosen? The knowledge and services of social science experts will be invaluable here. Psychologists familiar with the customs and ways of country A can be called upon to state the most typical personality traits and types to be found in that country and psychologists of country A can select or develop tests which disclose the best-known, national personality types of that country. Over and above everything else, selectees should be expected to be friendly towards country B and definitely interested in being able to live in it and move through it, once they are chosen as *temporary* residents for the goodwill enclave. Furthermore, they should be selectees who can be counted upon to be ambassadors of goodwill for country A. They should be allowed to be atypical of their home country only in the sense that they speak the language of the host country. The selection process can justifiably be biased in the sense that only the most appealing and friendly of country A's citizens should be chosen for residence in the to-be-transplanted enclave. The psychologists will also have to make certain that the leisure-time pursuits of the selectees, their interest profiles, their prevailing attitudes, their range of intelligence, education

---

[1] The reader can satisfy himself on this score by reading the following volume : Roy Lewis and Rosemary Stewart. *The Managers: A New Examination Of The English, German, & American Executive.* New York : Mentor Books, 1961. 256 pp.

and skills, and similar considerations, are typical of citizens of country A.

Sociologists will have to be consulted on the accuracy with which the social institutions and social processes which are to be designed into the prospective enclave are typical of country A. Political scientists will likewise have to be consulted with respect to the political institutions and processes that are characteristic of community life *at the local level* in country A. Economists will have to pass judgment on the accuracy of the work patterns and occupations to be reflected by the enclave and on the accuracy with which the numerical distribution of the occupations and professions of a typical, small community in country A have been designed into the prospective enclave. They will also have to pass judgment on which goods and services of the enclave may be stocked and supplied by the mother country, where such goods and services are dependent strictly upon the existing, large-scale technology of the mother country.

Both countries A and B must agree to establish representative, goodwill enclaves reciprocally. The funding of such enclaves should preferably come from the two countries involved, although some degree of financial support should probably be supplied by the United Nations. Each enclave should be open to visitation by citizens of the host country but only at *reasonable times* and in *reasonable numbers*, so as not to upset the ongoing life of the enclave community. The citizens of each enclave should be permitted to travel freely about the host country, so that they, too, will become familiar with the life and culture of the host country and, hopefully, learn of its virtues as well as its defects. Each host country should be free to pass judgment on the suitabi-

lity and acceptability of the representatives of the foreign country who are to constitute the citizens of the prospective enclave, in order to assure themselves that the goodwill enclave will not constitute a base of operations for espionage. A rotation principle should be permanently employed so that every few years a fraction of the enclave's citizens returns to the mother country and is replaced by a suitable, similar fraction of new representatives.

The citizens of any such enclave should possess a community newspaper, to be printed in the language of the host country, extra copies of which are made available to the libraries and schools of the host country, to members of the United Nations, various individuals and institutions of country A and to the politicians and statesmen of the host country who operate in its capital. It should also be made available to subscribers who may wish to receive it regularly on a financial basis. Such a community newspaper should be guaranteed freedom of the press and be encouraged not only to describe the life of its own community but should also be free to evaluate, criticize and comment upon the life of the host country. This community newspaper should be supported by other mass media of communication in the enclave, such as a radio and television station, a cinema which exhibits the best films of the mother country, lecture forums to which the citizens of the host country may be invited, sports events which are made available to a specified number of citizens of the host country on a free basis, and similar supporting activities. The goodwill enclave can also choose a body of its own citizens to act as agents to bring over performers in the arts from the mother country with admissions to performances made available to citizens and students of the host country in some cases on a paying basis and in others on a complimentary basis.

Another body of citizens in the enclave should be entrusted with the free choice of books from the mother country which are to be translated into the language of the host country and made available for distribution and sale to citizens of the host country. Furthermore, the advertising media of the host country should make space available on a paying basis, in order to bring such translated materials to the attention of a prospective reading public. Since the currency of the enclave community will be that of the mother country, all financial transactions should be on a cash or credit basis with the understanding that payments will be made in the currency of the host country and will be subject to the official exchange ratios. Domestic currency needed by enclave citizens when travelling about the host country will also be subject to official exchange ratios.

Citizens of an enclave should be free to attend not only their own schools but those of the host country. This should be particularly true for the children and young adults of families living in the enclave. Special transportation rates to travel to, and attend the cultural activities of, the host country and special admission rates to these activities, should be made available by the host country to the citizens of the enclave. Cultural activities which emphasize competition between enclave citizens and those of the host country—such as sports—should be minimized in order not to reinforce partisanship, xenophobia and polarization of group identifications, but these same cultural activities and sports can be made competitive through organized subgroups of citizens of the enclave itself, and citizens of the host country can be encouraged to attend these.

Every enclave should have an *ombudsman* of the host country who speaks the language of the enclave and who is friendly to, and knowledgeable about, the home country of the enclave's citizens. He should have two functions. The first should be that of representing his own country's views when its citizens feel that the members of the enclave are violating the hospitality and goodwill of the host country and they would like to see such violations—even if unintended—ended. The second should be that of representing the enclave's views before the host country, when the majority of the enclave's citizens feel they have been improperly treated by individual citizens or groups of the host country.

Clearly there are many other details of a goodwill enclave that can be spelled out. The important point, however, is to emphasize the fact that good-will enclaves which are reciprocated between two countries which are currently in conflict in a variety of ways, should help considerably to increase the amount of joint cultural understanding and goodwill between their respective citizens. Citizens of the enclave who return to their home country not only can be expected to act as ambassadors of goodwill for their former host country but they can also be counted upon to spread accurate information about that host country. In addition, this expectation can be reinforced by each country if it guarantees that its returning citizens will be free to maintain an organization and a newspaper which publishes friendly and knowledgeable articles about their former host country. If their home country guarantees both to fund such a newspaper and to distribute it where it will do the most good, this will maintain continuity of goodwill even after the emissaries return. If the emissary organization is further guaranteed access, by its own government, to mass media of communication for the development of programs aimed at promoting mutual, cultural understanding and goodwill, this removes the institution of the goodwill enclave from the realm of one-shot affairs. Finally, the strength of such emissary organizations is bound to increase with time because of the rotation principle I have clearly suggested.

3. An International Newspaper Under United Nations Auspices

Knowledgeable supporters of the UN, who pin a good deal of faith on the capacity of that body to create an increasing amount of international understanding and cross-cultural familiarity, are acquainted with the extent to which that organization publishes and sells books, periodicals and statistical and economic reports in English, French and Spanish, which are generally distributed throughout the world.[1] However, the one organ which might best cement international goodwill and understanding among the literate citizens of the world— namely, a common, international newspaper— has, to my knowledge, never been launched by the UN. One can look carefully through a popular volume, like that of Coyle,[2] describing the activities of the UN, or a more scholarly volume, like that of Ross,[3] and find no extended discussion of the value and feasibility of such a proposal. What are some of the difficulties in the way of establishing an international organ of this sort?

First, there is the so-called "language barrier." There is a common conviction that (1) because there exists no international language and (2) the representatives of different languages are reluctant to accede to the proposition that any *major* language other than their own should become a vehicle of popular, international communication, it is felt that it would be well-nigh impossible to establish such an international newspaper. Both of the two preceding assertions are quite true, but the conclusion is not. It is quite true that neither Esperanto, Ido, Volapük, Interglossa nor any of the other various proposals aimed at eliminating existing language barriers, have taken popular and widespread root in any country of the world. There are many reasons for this but one of them is surely human inertia. Even Basic English as proposed by C. K. Ogden has got nowhere and yet this linguistic invention would have required a vocabulary of less than 1000 words. As an abbreviated, second language to be introduced into all literate countries influenced by science, technology and international relations, Basic English would have required at most only a few months of training in elementary schools and could have been strongly reinforced subsequently with reading materials expressed in it, and distributed in classroom, library and cinema documentary. For all the preceding reasons it is a fact that we must record failure in the historical effort to establish an international language.

Likewise any international concession to the use of any major language, English or otherwise, is not to be expected in the light of existing cultural parochialisms—parochialisms which are intensified by the current atmosphere of international tensions. Furthermore, the representatives of most nations are convinced that the use of any single, existing, major language for purposes of international communication and, especially, as a vehicle for an international newspaper, would give a political and cultural advantage to those countries which spoke the major language in question. As a result, the major power blocs, whose leaders and representatives are certainly not saints, are not going to engage in a show of moral and social altruism

[1] Such publications are listed regularly in the periodical brochure produced by the UN, entitled *Monthly Sales Bulletin, Bulletin mensuel de ventes, Boletin Mensuel de Ventas,* issued by the Sales Section of the UN, New York.

[2] David Cushman Coyle. *The United Nations And How It Works.* New York: Mentor Books, 1960. Fifth Printing. 222 pp.

[3] Alf Ross. *The United Nations: Peace And Progress.* Totawa, New Jersey: *The Bedminster Press,* 1966. 443 pp.

and make the needed concession to an existing major language as the proper vehicle for international communication. We need, therefore, not quarrel with the second point either, since it is both well established and well taken.

However, it should be pointed out that all criticisms in terms of the language barrier—even though true—are somewhat wide of the mark. This is because any international newspaper to be published under UN auspices *does not have to be published in a single language*. In fact, it would be even more desirable to have an international newspaper which was published in *several* major languages or—for that matter—in most of the better known languages used throughout the world. This is precisely one of the easier possibilities that are open to us in the light of the many multilingual experts now available throughout the world and in the face of the fact that there are many excellent translators now associated with the UN, who could preside over the needed translation function with ease. A UN international newspaper, launched in several currently existing languages, must regard its major task as that of *uniformly* presenting world news and opinion as the members of the UN themselves view events and the clash of personal and social values. The uniformity of which I speak refers to the duty of presenting the same facts in a UN newspaper, even though these facts have to be put before the reader in different languages. Likewise that uniformity demands that the clash of national opinion, cultural outlooks and bloc preferences, be honestly set before the reader and set before him clearly and fully, no matter in what language he may be reading about them. In short, a UN international newspaper must take pains to ensure that all world citizens are *made familiar with the same facts and the same spectrum of opinion*. The presentation of such material, however, definitely *does not require* that all citizens read about it *in the same language*. Thus, it can be seen that in this sense the publication of an international UN newspaper would be both feasible and desirable.

It is not really the language which would be important for an international newspaper which is to be launched under UN auspices. Rather *it would be the content*, that is to say, the actual news and opinions that would be furnished by such a paper. Even if we agree that *content* is what is important rather than the use of a single language, nevertheless we run into another set of difficulties. There will not be many differences concerning the *facts* of international *issues* and *disputes*, since these can be established *in principle* by bodies of experts attached to the UN organization itself. There will, however, be frequent differences of opinion concerning *the interpretation of facts*. The recognition of this latter eventuality is then used by some people as an argument against the feasibility of an international newspaper. This infeasibility is argued on the grounds that it would be impossible for the editors of a UN newspaper—or the membership of that body as a whole, itself—to achieve any agreement on the interpretation of the legal, moral, social, economic or cultural considerations that surround the international issues of our time. These issues are rooted in international tensions and these tensions are, themselves, generators of further tensions.

But, once again, we are facing an argument which is wide of the mark. The purpose of a UN international newspaper would not be to present a united front of agreement of international, controversial matters or to provide a monolithic homogeneity of opinions. The point of an international newspaper is precisely to present those congeries of conflicting opinion which *actually exists among members of the UN and among the citizens and leaders of the world's nations*. It is these conflicts in opinion which should be made available, in their native languages, to the citizens of all countries. These citizens would find that the UN international newspaper made available to them all sides on a given issue. The whole point of an international newspaper is to provide the citizens of the world—and particularly those who are sympathetic to the cause of world government—with the prevailing differences of opinion on international issues, so that they make up their own minds as to where they choose to stand and which of the alternatives among proposed solutions to problems they would prefer. It is the latter desideratum which can be expected to encourage the increasing acceptability of useful compromise and establish workable and satisfying consensus of give and take.

At present each national sovereignty presents chiefly its own position to its citizens. Where it presents the position of opposing national groups on a conflicting issue, it not only tends to give an incomplete presentation of the opposing side but it also tends to slant the interpretation of that side, to present it as weakly as possible and to give relatively little opportunity for rebuttal. An international newspaper, under UN auspices, will allow each nation to present its position in the strongest possible light. Then, and only then, can an enlightened and informed world opinion arise. Then, and only then, will an international poll of sentiment be meaningful. The results of such an opinion poll on issues facing the UN will, of course, never be binding. However, we can expect that both nations and their representatives at the UN will increasingly take stock of such enlightened and informed opinion and act in terms of it. Unquestionably a result of this sort is one major way in which international understanding and cooperation can receive expression.

To whom would such an international newspaper be distributed, once it is funded by the UN? It would go to national statesmen and politicians, to schools and libraries, to the leaders of various organizations such as churches, trade unions, political parties, civic bodies, regular newspapers, etc. Leaders of such organizations and institutions will always be free to duplicate for their members any particular issue of the international newspaper, using their own financial resources. This will be made easy by liberally exercised permission procedures in which the UN copyright is exercised only to ensure accurate reproduction and quotation of material from the international newspaper. Distortion of its material can be checked by making such distortion subject to fine and public correction over the mass media of communication of each country as a courtesy service. Each nation would also have the privilege of funding the reproduction of any issue of such an international newspaper, particularly if it seeks to distribute it on a wider scale. Under no circumstances, however, should the cost of any such *national* printing and distribution burden be made part of the operating budget of the UN.

I submit, then, that the inauguration of such an institution as a UN newspaper is certain to increase the fund of international understanding and goodwill. It would be a considerably useful device for enabling men to understand and appreciate differences in cultures and ways of life. It could not help but enlarge the compass of human understanding as it succeeded with the passage of time in acquainting world citizens with widespread social psychologies quite different from their own. At the same time it would provide the citizens of the world with a common exposition of the world's problems rather than just those of their own country. It would bring into focus for all readers the nature of existing international issues and the variety of solutions proposed for dealing with them.

Finally, it will also give readers an opportunity to express themselves on all these matters— before a clearing-house body of some sort, set up in the UN—through letters and telegrams. This opportunity would admittedly be fraught with some risk for citizens who identify themselves by letter, telegram or cablegram, who happen to be living under totalitarian regimes which are made unhappy by minority views. Such regimes could also round up fictitious letter writers and telegram and cablegram dispatchers, in order to give the appearance of a national public sentiment which, in fact, does not exist. Even these risks, however, are amenable to gradual reduction as time goes on, if political scientists are willing to give some thought to developing measures and means by which the authenticity of messages can be established and the risk to citizens of retaliation by their governments be reduced practically to zero. In any event the expression of opinion by newspaper readers from the world's non-totalitarian regimes will be almost wholly free of risk and this would be a desirable first step on the way to global freedom of opinion and global understanding and enlightenment.

Contemporary Economic Dehumanization: Some Difficulties Surrounding Its Reduction

Many social scientists, like the Vatican's Father De Lestapis, Dr. Mukerjee of India, and Great Britain's Lord Simon of Wythenshaw, have pointed out the dehumanizing results of a situation in which by 1980, the US, with 9.5 percent of the world's population, will be consuming, at the present rate, 83 percent of its raw materials. The present paper represents an attempt to show the difficult problems which are associated with the effort to reduce such dehumanization.

THE folly of our foreign policy of containment of Communist expansionism and the opposed mystique of the Communists—that Marxist concepts of community are the seeds of the future and that Sino-Soviet expansion is merely the midwife for the birth pangs of the classless society to come—can be best seen, I believe, in relation to the cryptic concern which really underlies both these approaches to international tensions. That concern is a matter which is rarely the focus of attention at the conference table. I am referring to the need for a more equitable distribution of the resources of the globe, both on land and under the sea. In this connection, I wish to emphasize the fact that basically the technologically advanced countries have no moral right to assume that nature's bounty was intended primarily as their breadbasket. Their privileged position in this respect is a matter of economic "squatter sovereignty," itself a historical accident.

One must emphasize that the immorality reflected in the fact that the technologically advanced countries, whose populations constitute 13 percent of the world's inhabitants, take it for granted morally that they are entitled to 55 percent of the world's income or—to put the matter more starkly—the world's wealth and resources. Americans and West Europeans—and certainly Americans more than West Europeans—live high off the hog precisely because they take the wealth from other people's back yards and use it for themselves. We tend to regard the natural resources of industrially underdeveloped countries as a storehouse of raw materials for purposes of maintaining and improving our own standard of living. Any questions concerning the rectitude of this assumption rarely cross our minds. The Soviets are, of course, equally guilty of the same attitude, but they are not always so successful

SOCIAL SCIENCE, 1967, vol. 42, 80-85.

as we are in giving it concrete expression. I am referring to such facts as the Soviet effort to make a satellite country like Rumania specialize in the direction of becoming an agricultural supplier to the Soviet Union. The USSR, of course, failed in this objective. Rumanian leadership thumbed its nose at the Soviet Union and decided to become an economic mix of industry and agriculture and has begun to move toward expanded industrialization.

The peoples of the world and particularly The Third World—that group of countries (of which India, Indonesia, South and Central America are representative) whose inhabitants constitute 64 percent of the world's total population but who command only 19 percent of the world's income—have as much moral right to life, liberty, and the pursuit of happiness as the nations of the West. To try to preserve the economic status quo by looking upon them as raw-material "feeders" to the industrially advanced nations of the West is a form of cryptic dehumanization. The willingness of Western citizens to permit the continuation of the economic exploitation of industrially underdeveloped countries is the international analogue of that form of alienation by which the worker in a Western factory becomes indifferent to the social effects of the things he helps to fabricate. The Western industrial worker rarely sees the customer, rarely sees the distant social effects of what he has produced, and is rarely acquainted with any of the terminal dehumanizing effects of his output. So he can continue to work with an easy conscience and a swollen but socially approved lack of social responsibility. In the same way, the economic and social havoc wrought upon underdeveloped nations by the cryptic dehumanization of unequal access to the economic dinner table is marginal to the moral consciousness of Western man.

To correct this economic dehumanization and inequity, we need, bluntly speaking, a reallocation of the earth's resources. By this we mean access to both natural resources and technological resources (capital stock and equipment). This access can be made possible either through money loaned, as an outright gift, or through some up-to-date form of lend-lease. We need a system of international priorities and allocations—one which will redress what Western man has wrought. Only in this way can the economic and social dehumanization of the present age be reversed.

Yet even if all the have-nations of the world were to sit down tomorrow in an act of superb Christian charity, and agree to reallocate the resources of the earth—to humanize these resources, so to speak—they would face tremendous difficulties. These difficulties are the social costs inherent in the complex international interrelationships which have now woven together such factors as national trade, national industrial capacity, national annual rate of population growth, and national standard of living. In order to indicate the problems which would attend the institutional expression of a Christian humanization and morality, reflected in the secular terms of trade, economics, and industrialization, let me discuss some of the difficulties which would accompany any international resolution to humanize nature's bounty equitably.

If the nations of the world were to agree to a reallocation of the earth's resources, they would still have to face the following problems. How shall we decide which of the advanced nations must undergo, for the first time in recent history, a voluntary technological cutback? Such a cutback, in spite of its altruistic intentions, would, itself, produce some dehumanizing effects in terms of unemployment, financial losses, and so forth, and the personal and social dislocations such factors inevitably produce. What is the extent of the technologically induced dehumanization in the technologically advanced countries which is to be put up with, in the effort to humanize access elsewhere to planetary resources? A technological cutback would imply the voluntary acceptance of increased and unused industrial capacity which is to be thrust upon advanced nations, and this in turn would be equivalent to a deliberate decision to waste valuable capital investment. A technological cutback for an advanced nation like the United States automatically reduces her topdog status, economically and politically speaking, throughout the world.

Nevertheless, such an eventuality would be inescapable unless we found that certain other alternatives of industrial humanization were open to us. Let us consider one of these. It might be agreed upon to allow the advanced nations to retain their industrial capacity but only by reversing the currently existing "feeder" effects, economically speaking. What would such a reversal mean? It would mean that, instead of raw materials flowing to a country like the USA and finished goods being produced, intended primarily for our domestic market and very secondarily for export, the emphasis on the destination of finished goods would be reversed. In a somewhat different sense, it is the United States and other technologically advanced countries which would have to become "feeder stations." Goods would then be intended primarily for the foreign market (the 64 percent of the world's inhabitants who are economically poor) and very secondarily for the domestic market. I am here assuming that the population of The Third World would be allowed to approach the American standard of living over, say, two or three decades.

Although this alternative would reverse our currently existing economic dehumanization, it would also result in economic dependency for presently existing have-not nations and would therefore be morally degrading. Furthermore, it would create a new type of dehumanization, one which deliberately laid down a policy which, by implication, would prevent the industrial development of The Third World—a form of curtailment which one might christen "developmental dehumanization." Considering the present state of man's moral development and the stunted aspects of social altruism which the profit motive produces in the West, it is also true that it is not very likely that the inhabitants of technologically advanced countries would consent to working hard to feed the world and to supply it with consumer goods and services, apart from food. To do so would result in permitting a more humane mode of work in the economically backward countries, while the inhabitants of the technologically advanced countries would be working harder than ever before. This would probably be regarded as a form of dehumanization in reverse.

In addition, such an alternative would dehumanize the socioeconomic conditions for posterity. With the whole world consuming raw materials at a rate which rapidly approached that consonant with the United States standard of living, this would be equivalent to exhausting irreplaceable resources that will be vitally needed by future generations. This is economic dehumanization exported over time. A contingency of this sort is not very likely to be prevented by the coming technologies of seafarming and seamining, because these will probably not be developed at a rate which will make it economically feasible to expect them to be able to assume the major share of the production responsibilities of a world which has decided to expand economic good cheer more equitably.

The truth of the matter, then, appears to be that for a proper expression of the Christian spirit in the matter of the reallocation of planetary resources—a reallocation which will involve a more equitable distribution nationally and regionally—the technologically and economically advanced nations may have to take only a moderate reduction in their standard of living. At the same time, the economically backward nations may have to recognize rather early that they can at best climb only toward such a more moderate and reduced Western standard of living. This more moderate standard of living would then become a bench mark for the economies of The Third World. In short, a global system of priorities and allocations with respect primarily to natural resources—and secondarily with respect to capital stock and equipment—would not only control which nation got what and when, but would also have to be used to determine the rate at which the injections of new income (or goods and services) could occur.

Nor would this be the only complication staring an economically well-intentioned and humanized Western Christianity in the face. In order to make the allocations of goods and services meaningful—even though these were variable over time—one would have to prescribe mandatory, differential birth rates for the various countries of the world. This procedure would be inescapable because the rate of capital expansion created for the poor countries, and the rate at which they would require goods and services in relation to a specified standard of living, would both be indissolubly linked to national and regional population growth rates. Given a prescribed standard of living as a national objective, given the rate of capital expansion needed to meet such a standard of living, given the rate of resource utilization such capital equipment would require if operated a specified number of hours per day, then these constraints must automatically involve by implication a specifiable maximum population increase. If we assume that mortality rates can be approximately equalized everywhere throughout the world, then changes in population growth will be due basically to changes in birth rate. The allowable population maximum can be expressed in terms of a maximum allowable annual growth rate. This, in turn, complicates the process of family formation, family size, and similar considerations.

The worst feature of such a humanizing innovation is the fact that we can formulate neither a rational nor a moral basis for prescribing differential national population growth rates. Yet we must establish such differential growth rates in order to meet the considerations entailed in a Christian expression of the desire to share nature's bounty more equitably. This would be one of the most paralyzing blockages of all. No one to date has given thought to the formulation of a metaphysics which could establish required national differentials in growth rates—differentials which are inescapably tied to the process of economic humanization and redistribution of the planet's wealth. This arises from the fact that the prorating of global wealth, in terms of a process of economic humanization, precedes the problem of population control. This would be in contrast to the present treatment of the demographic problem of alleviating national population explosions, in which we ask that birth rates be controlled in relation to ongoing resources and the current state of technological development in a given country or area.

Although, in both the situation we are envisaging and the current demographic one, we must adjust birth rates to what we have, nevertheless the former differs from the latter in one major respect. In the former case, what we have could change radically from one year to the next, since a metaphysics governing just, and unjust proposals for redistribution may be of such a nature as to encourage large leaps or cutbacks from time to time. What we would have can therefore be subject to violent fluctuations and discontinuities. This, of course, can rarely happen in the process of natural economic growth, for such growth is typically not subject to huge injections or withdrawals of capital goods and equipment or of raw materials. But under a moral metaphysics of redistribution, such huge and sudden injections will clearly be permissible.

Such injections would, of course, probably create a population growth lag in relation to a specified standard of living, a raising and thereby a violation of the consensually agreed upon standard of living, or the establishment of a larger, ever normal granary and material resource pool than was formerly thought to be justified. A curtailment or withdrawal of part of previously redistributed produce—which would occasionally occur as a result of previous planning errors of one sort or another—would result in a reduced standard of living. Such reduction would automatically have to fall below the agreed upon level. If this did not occur, then the birth rate would have to be allowed to fall below the level previously prescribed. In all these situations, the effort to humanize the redistribution of wealth and opportunity could become messy, indeed.

Men have never before faced the problems of economic humanization in terms of allocation of resources to large and fixed national or cultural groups. If population growth rates were not coordinated to redistributed global gross national product—consensually agreed upon internationally—then priorities and allocations would certainly become meaningless, for the more an actual population growth rate exceeded an assigned one, the greater would be the debit in the previously rendered resource allocation which had been made in relation to a specified standard of living. Any nation which refused under these circumstances to control its annual rate of population increase would, in effect, be going on a wildcat strike, demographically speaking. Such strikes would make it impossible to humanize the world economically in terms of a more just redistribution of the world's wealth.

All the preceding points then indicate in brief compass some of the problems which men must face if they wish to work against the presently existing economic dehumanization of the world. If, therefore, humanists of every vintage desire to see their ideals receive expression beyond merely the programmatic stage, they have two major responsibilities, apart from the existential responsibility of describing current human folly and insensitivity and the manner in which these produce some of the major social pathology of our time. In addition to the process of calling a spade a spade, humanists would have to make themselves knowledgeable with respect to the social complexity of our age. In this way, and only in this way, can they earn a view of what Aristotle called "the art of the possible." Only by understanding the "go" and structure produced by the artifacts of man's own creation—economically, technologically, socially, legally, and so forth—can they relate the economic dehumanization which they would like to abjure to the institutions and processes which generate it.

Even more important than this, however, is the responsibility humanists must face of having to learn to frame proposals which could liquidate the existing social pathology which arouses their ire. Such a demand may, perhaps, seem too unreasonable for beings confined to a single lifetime. In that case, then, humanists should, at least, be prepared to be knowledgeable enough to evaluate the proposals which others formulate for economically humanizing the world. This function of creative social and economic humanization is one which, it seems to me, is indispensable if classical humanism is to be transformed into an effective *Weltanschauung* for the needs of an age dominated—at least externally—by science and technology.

These additional responsibilities must be assumed by those who wish to march under the banner of humanism and who wish to see the humanistic *Weltanschauung* given concrete expression in our age. The tasks of economic humanization are very demanding. A transformed humanism, academically speaking, is now in order. Let us hope that we can look forward during the next decade to educational and cultural expressions of this transformation. The economic humanization of the planet, we believe, will be considerably advanced by humanistic modes of consciousness of the type we have emphasized here.

PART III: VISION AND VIEWPOINT

IN THE HUMAN CONDITION

AT THE CROSSROADS OF SOCIAL RENEWAL
NO VISION WILL KEEP

The Relationship Between Commitment and Development

Human development is always a product of commitment. The quality of a community's way of life is, of course, substantially dependent upon the vision of its members. But that vision means little if it does not receive concrete expression in the activities of men. It is these activities that fall under the generic rubric of "commitment." Almost all men dedicate themselves to ideals which do not allow sufficiently for social change. They pursue commitments that unwittingly attempt to fix the condition of man for all time. Yet no vision will provide a seedbed either for all human potentialities or emerging contingencies. This is a sufficiently depressing thought unto itself. Yet even more depressing is the fact that men are also unaware of—or, when aware—indifferent to, the inhumane and undesirable features of their current commitments. Here, too, some contemporary vision is often allowed to dam up the waves of social change. The winds of doctrine become more important than the social damage they produce. The social and moral insufficiencies of ideas which straitjacket and circumscribe our lives are ignored.

The Socratic injunction to the effect that the unexamined life is not worth living has never really entered deeply into the secular affairs of men. We give lip service to visions which we honor more in the breach than in the observance. At other times
HUMANITAS, Feb. 1972, vol. 8, #1, 97-117.

we fulfill visions to the letter and when it becomes obvious that these fulfillments have entered into a marriage partnership with Original Sin, we ignore the morally and socially reprehensible issue of the marriage. Our attitudes seem to say, "Well I've got mine, so to hell with what's happening." And thus, through the domination of our basest impulses, we become silent partners to the transformation of our society into a Hobbesian world. In such a world, each of us is on his own and in a mad scramble for personal happiness and security, the attitude of all is summed up in the old adage "After me, the deluge."

The visions that men live by carry the seeds of their own destruction. The commitments in action by which men honor these visions all too often unwittingly produce evil in their wake. We have few forms of social accounting that take stock of the damage thus produced—at least not until it is almost too late. We show so much value-inertia that we refuse to examine closely the inconsistencies and the evil consequences that may be inherent in the high-level abstractions through which we express and execute our visions. We become alienated from the tragedies these dreams sow all about us. Thus we enlarge the cemetery of our soon-to-be-buried dreams and transform our commitments into comic operas for the gods.

In this paper, I should like to examine *some* of the visions which currently move men and indicate some of the pathological features inherent in them. In this way, perhaps, we can check somewhat the tendency to commit ourselves uncritically to visions whose effects—if these visions are permitted unchecked, social expression— will destroy much that we value. Visions not examined critically may function like the broom of the sorcerer's apprentice, lying about here and there, sweeping up much that we value, while we find ourselves unable to put to rest the broom's frantic activities. Our visions must be tools, not crutches—tools to be discarded when they have outlived their usefulness. The successful, but usually temporary, expression of a vision via the institutions that we develop should not be seen as the equivalent of gaining entrance to Paradise. Let me then turn to the role of vision and commitment in human experience.

Vision One : Capitalism

The initial vision of the free enterprise system was that if every man sought his own economic ends, the general welfare would be served. The intelligence, the talents and the cunning of the entrepreneur, it was argued, would improve the material condition of all. In addition, it was further asserted, that for exercising his abilities on behalf of the general run of men, man was entitled to a substantial reward for his labors in the form of profits. Basically, capitalism did not erect greed and selfishness into virtues. Instead, their energies were made productive and deflected to social purposes. Dedication to the capitalist system recognized that there was less profit in morally condemning the self-seeking propensities of the human animal than in making those propensities work for others at the same time that they worked for oneself.

The capitalist *ethos* glorified competition. The Christian spirit, in contrast, made a virtue out of cooperation. Christian, economic man tolerated the contradiction in silence. The capitalist theoretician condemned the lazy and saw the plight of the economically unfortunate as one which the unfortunate had brought on themselves by their own improvidence. Social Darwinism was a natural, first mate on the capitalist ship. If the lifetime efforts and savings of a businessman were liquidated by the price and cost pressures of the market, the apologist for capitalism shed not a tear. After all, this was an inefficient producer and he deserved his fate. That was part of the order of things and the name of the game was competition. Some rose, some sunk, and that was all there was to it. That industrial coalitions could be formed to ruin a producer was a fact ignored or lightly rationalized in the atmosphere of competition. To those devoted to capitalism, no greater, more practical and more virtuous institution than competition had ever been devised by the mind of men. That cooperation had also been able successfully to meet human needs—both economic and non-economic—and create the conditions for progress, as Kropotkin[1] has shown, was a fact to which the advocates of free enterprise were really indifferent.

[1] Peter Kropotkin. *Mutual Aid: A Factor Of Evolution.* Boston: Porter Sargent, n.d.

With the advent of a technology that moved Western man from an economy of scarcity to an economy of abundance, the purist vision of traditional, Western capitalism became absurd and required the most tortured rationalizations for its defense. Bazelon[2] has painted a picture of some of the newer institutional forms by which the older, absurd vision is now disguised. Few listened. Kelso and Adler[3] have tried to preserve the traditional vision by increasing the base of ownership through equity-sharing plans and thereby reducing the current inequities in the distribution of wealth. The ideas they advocate have made little dent. Few aspects of current, economic realities correspond to the traditional assumptions of the free-enterprise system. Yet that which is non-existent is currently defended, as Arnold[4] so succinctly and amusingly has shown, by dead symbols, comical myths and a folklore to which nearly everyone is susceptible. Nothing is able to burst the iridescent bubble into which the traditional vision has been transformed.

But the preceding criticisms touch chiefly upon the moral insufficiencies of the capitalist vision. Partisans of capitalism were also relatively indifferent to many of the *social costs* of private enterprise. A limited spectrum of these has been dealt with by Kapp.[5] Here it is sufficient to point out that the glories of competition have produced such important, social side-effects as extended unemployment, economic insecurity, occupational obsolescence, poverty for those lacking the talents or training to meet the skills demanded by industry, enforced retirement and economic isolation for individuals who are often still useful, productive and creative, and the truncation of their standard of living through inflation. Morally, competition and the need of workers for job security has, in fact, created an economically coercive atmosphere in which the average worker is a wage slave. In turn, wage slavery has also deprived the worker of many non-

[2]David T. Bazelon. *The Paper Economy.* New York: Random House, 1963.

[3]Louis O. Kelso and Mortimer J. Adler. *The Capitalist Manifesto.* New York: Random House, 1958.

[4]Thurman Arnold. *The Folklore Of Capitalism.* New Haven: Yale University Press, 1959.

[5]K. William Kapp. *The Social Costs Of Private Enterprise.* Cambridge, Massachusetts: Harvard University Press, 1950.

economic forms of autonomy. Many of these forms of autonomy were second nature to the craftsmen who were our forbears in that long-ago period preceding the industrial revolution. Many non-economic contexts of behavior are linked to the worker's economic sphere and he risks managerial displeasure and job deprivation were he to make certain types of fateful decisions and choices in these non-economic contexts. In this way the erosion of his autonomy is assured.

Social costs such as these, and others I have not mentioned, are a direct burden upon the worker in the system of free enterprise. But the rest of us, the consumers, are deeply affected by other social costs that are even more important than the depressing job atmosphere in which so many workers must labor. These other social costs consist of the whole train of environmental pathologies directly connected with production under capitalism—environmental pathologies to whose creation management may be socially indifferent and to whose elimination management may be morally indifferent. These are now all matters about which we are nationally conscious. These environmental pathologies include such elements as the following: air and water pollution, soil degradation, soil leaching and soil poisoning, chemicals used in agriculture and food processing, "animal factories" used in the large-scale raising of cattle and poultry, the wanton and unnecessary killing of life and the alienated destruction of growing things, the problem of waste disposal, the abuse and misuse of man's technology, and the inappropriate use of chemotherapy in medicine in relation to physiological functioning viewed as a complex system of inter-locking biological equilibra. These are, however, merely the widespread, *physical* pathologies of environmental degradations.

But there are other types of ecological upset. The phrase, "environmental pathology," can also be used in connection with the degradation of city life, via noise and congestion, the stresses of modern, urban-industrial civilization, and all the cultural and socio-psychological intangibles that are part of man's "spiritual nutrition." Likewise the term, "environment," can also be reasonably applied to artifacts, materials and transformations man introduces into the atmosphere, such as small metal particles in space, the debris of space rockets and communications satellites, radiation, sonic booms, excess carbon dioxide, toxic children's toys, dangerous, household appliances, and so on. Finally, with equal justice, the term, "environment," can be used in connection with the transformations man creates in the marine biosphere, such as oil slicks on the ocean's surface, waste and sewage brought by outfalls and garbage scows increasingly further from our shores, cylinders of nerve gas buried at sea which, if they ever lose their content to their surroundings, will probably create significant changes in the ocean's ecology, sunken vessels that may still contain enormous and live, explosive materials.

In all these senses, then, the term, "environment," can legitimately point to many foci far beyond the major ones that we usually visualize in connection with air and water pollution and waste disposal. It is inescapable that these meanings will be extended with the progress of science and technology. It is the need to alert ourselves to the many extensions of the meaning of the term, "environment," that is now a civic responsibility we owe to ourselves.

One could, of course, launch into an extended discussion of all the preceding elements of environmental pathology, the ways in which they are encouraged by the visions of the merits of free enterprise, and the wastes, losses and sufferings bound up with them. One could, likewise, go into detail on several other undesirable, social costs and consequences that have been produced by the vision of the merits of a system of free enterprise. Such ventures would be both unnecessary and beside the point. The point is that today the vision of what has been called the capitalistic system needs to be either drastically overhauled or actually supplanted by a new vision. This would have to be a vision of a social and economic order that will provide the material benefits of technology for a mass society, without exacting as a price the many pathological, social costs which we are now enduring. The early vision of the benefits of free enterprise was an abstract one. It was a vision that too largely ignored much of the social fabric that lay outside of economics proper. Today what was ignored in the past by textbook economics is being revived as a true concern of the present, by some of our younger, radical economists.[6] In any event, the traditional vision of the advantages of capitalism was embedded in a real world that is no longer with us. Technological change, social change, demographic change and ecological change have all conspired to make that vision both irrelevant, false and harmful.

That vision will no longer keep and, because this is so, commitment to it *in its traditional form* is likely to prove a lengthy frustration. The next phases of human development will probably eclipse the capitalist vision entirely, as Whyte[7] seems to think. In any event, we have to move on.

[6]See the following article that deals briefly with the ideas and activities of those younger, academic economists who belong to the new organization known as the *Union for Radical Political Economics* (URPE). Melville J. Ulmer, "Economics on the New Left: More Than Marxist," *The New Republic*, Vol. 163, No. 26, December 26, 1970, pp. 13-14. Among the critiques of modern economics made by the URPE are the following: (1) economics and institutional economists are reactionary and part of an economic and social elite that will not encourage radical analysis of the ongoing realities of our economic system; and (2) the concept of GNP is too full of undesirable defects to be a trustworthy indicator of whether our material lot is improving or deteriorating and among these defects is the dollar value of all "illth" created in the U.S., unnecessary pollution and unnecessary waste and other forms of *negative* production. Ulmer has this to say:

> Other topics that occupy the new left are the economic exploitation of women, the economic role of war and the real cost of the Vietnam conflict, the economics of racial discrimination, the nature of "competition" among monopolies, the correction of statistical fallacies bearing on the distribution of income, and the role played in environmental pollution by planned obsolescence and by vested interests (such as the automobile industry's opposition to mass transportation). The new left is also concerned with the current dilemma of economic instability, and, unlike the prevailing orthodoxy, would go well beyond the "new economics" and jawboning in seeking correctives. A majority of the radicals would likewise go farther than most liberals in removing inequities in the distribution of income . . . (p. 14).

[7]Lancelot Law Whyte. *The Next Development In Man.* New York: Mentor Books, 1962.

Roadblocks to the Fulfillment of the Democratic Vision

I cannot devote separate space to the vision of socialism (or communism). It is not that that vision has been tried and found wanting. Rather, as G.B. Shaw remarked somewhere, it has never been tried at all. Communism in the USSR has not proved to be a first step on the road to Utopia. A vast literature attests to the dismal failure of communism, wherever it has been tried, and because a reader can hardly turn around without contacting books and periodical literature on the subject of this failure, I am not going to name-drop in this area. But these skimpy remarks are no criticism of the vision of socialism, itself, which has not, as yet, been put fully into practice anywhere on earth. There are, however, many who are still committed to this old vision, but in forms in which it is critically examined for its relevance as a framework for a mass society based upon science and technology. One finds expressions of this commitment in the writings of those who contribute to such journals as *Dissent*[8] and *The New Leader*,[9] in individually authored books by such intellectual sophisticates as the French, radical philosopher, Gorz,[10] the Yugoslav philosopher, Petrović,[11] and in the older, more classical, but penetrating criticism by the French sociologist, Durkheim.[12] One likewise finds renewed effort to restate the socialist vision for the technological society of the twentieth century in a famous position paper, published by the British organization, *Socialist Union*.[13] Finally, one also finds excellent collections of fresh and more

[8]*Dissent*, A Quarterly Of Socialist Opinion, is edited by Irving Howe. It is published by the Dissent Publishing Association, 509 Fifth Avenue, New York 17, New York.

[9]*The New Leader* is published by the American Labor Conference on International Affairs, Inc. The editorial and executive office is at 7 E. 15th Street, New York 3, N.Y.

[10]Andre Gorz. *Strategy For Labor: A Radical Proposal*. Translated from the French by Martin A. Nicolaus and Victoria Ortiz. Boston: Beacon Press, 1964.

[11]Gajo Petrović. *Marx In The Mid-Twentieth Century: A Yugoslav Philosopher Considers Karl Marx's Writings*. Garden City, New York: Doubleday, 1967.

[12]Emile Durkheim. *Socialism*. Edited with an Introduction by Alvin W. Gouldner. New York: Collier Books, 1962.

[13]*Socialist Union. Twentieth Century Socialism. The Economy Of Tomorrow*. Harmondsworth, Middlesex: Penguin Books, 1956.

critical thinking about the socialist vision, in volumes edited by Mills[14] and Fromm.[15] Thus, it must be emphasized that there now also exists a literature of renascence for the socialist vision and it is only proper to refer the reader to that literature. Much of what I shall have to say about other visions, in the paragraphs which follow, will, of course, apply with equal force to the socialist vision, but I shall devote no separate and explicit remarks here to this vision itself.

I prefer, instead, to deal with some older and newer visions, commitment to which, in my opinion, is doomed to founder for a variety of reasons. One of these older visions is democracy, itself, and I should like to take a fresh look at this old vision—stretching from the Greeks to our own age—chiefly with a view to bringing into focus the reasons why dedication to its credo carries the seed of prospective failure.

Democracy, as originally conceived, is failing for a number of reasons. The two reasons chiefly emphasized in much of the existing literature that is critical of democracy, are the complexity of modern society and voter apathy. A good portion of the latter, of course, derives from the impossibility of achieving understanding and making decisions, as a result of the former condition, itself. There are many aspects to the concept of "social complexity" in a technologically based society like our own. I have discussed these elsewhere.[16] Here it will be sufficient if we think of social complexity in a general way in terms of only two considerations. The first of these is the sheer *difficulty* for the average citizen—and, for that matter, for many of our above-average citizens—of achieving an understanding of certain social concepts, social processes and social relationships. The second is the extra-ordinary amount of information required to achieve a genuine understanding of the nature of many of our problems,

[14]C. Wright Mills. *The Marxists*. New York: Dell, 1962. This book includes selections from leading Marxists of the past as well as critical exposition by C. Wright Mills himself.

[15]Erich Fromm (ed.) *Socialist Humanism: An International Symposium*. Garden City, New York: Doubleday, 1966.

[16]Henry Winthrop. *Ventures In Social Interpretation*. New York: Appleton-Century-Crofts, Inc., 1968. See in particular Part III, Chapters 12-16, inclusive, pp. 199-272.

their genesis, the structural aspects of the institutional procedures employed to deal with them, and the economic processes and legislative sanctions that govern them. The first taxes intellectual capacity considerably. The second is always a strain upon memory and attention-span.

Populist myths and the narcissism of grass-roots attitudes towards the true nature of the modern community tend to reinforce the already existing and uncritical egocentricity by which we hide the preceding truths from ourselves. But if the considerations already stressed were false to fact, it would then be both incongruous and ludicrous to emphasize the intensive training for knowledge, understanding and skill that we demand of the undergraduate in higher education and that we expect of those who are preparing to enter the professions. Our civilization is based upon science and technology. An authentic grasp of the essentials of scientific method is surely not possible within the range of ability of most of those individuals who fall within the 50 percent of the population with IQ's below 100. To assert this unpleasant truth is neither a cryptic form of intellectual snobbery nor a disguised form of educational elitism.

It is chiefly through scientific method that we discover truth, whether it be natural or social truth, and it is through scientific method that we are most cogently and clearly able to analyze the nature of the problems that beset us. That method now includes some knowledge of elementary, mathematical reasoning, some knowledge of the fundamentals of statistics and logic, and such newer modes of analysis as systems theory, operations research and input-output analysis. All of these clearly lie outside the grasp of the average citizen, although they are absolutely essential if we wish to understand how fruitful are conflicting and competing proposals for an attack upon our social problems. We demand the skills of those who enter the worlds of business and management. Our citizens expect these same skills of those who enter economics and other social science areas. We cannot, in good faith and in the spirit of common sense, expect the citizen to do without them in dealing with the social context of our lives—a context in which the existing problems are even more difficult to understand than those in business, and certainly less manageable.

If, therefore, the vote, the referendum, the citizen study group, and similar devices, are to be meaningful and effective, either in forms of representative or participatory democracy, the features of scientific method must become somewhat familiar to the citizen. But—and this is a recognizably tragic fact of political life—the *average citizen* is intellectually disfranchised from understanding them. While this state of affairs continues, his political activity and decision making is not likely to be very meaningful or effective. In fact, it is likely to be disastrous, to others as well as to himself.

What we have said about the intellectual skills required to understand the socially complex problems of our age is equally true for the minimum range of information required of the citizen. Without the information that is essential for an understanding of his milieu, he may be said to be *in this world but not of it*. He needs to know something about the findings of modern science and technology. He needs to know a little something about medicine but, even more important, also about public health and hygiene. Above all, a better understanding of the characteristics of spaceship earth, in an ecological sense, in a *sine qua non* for his further civic and political progress. For successful adaptation to a modern, socially complex milieu, he should also have a minimal familiarity with international relationships and trade, with corporate law, tax legislation, social accounting as well as business accounting, the rules of parliamentary procedure, the elements of investment and finance, and similar considerations too numerous to mention here. The average citizen is clearly ignorant on almost all of these matters.

Is it any wonder, then, that the democratic vision is failing and must continue to founder even more seriously as time passes? The social complexity which I have already emphasized, forces democracy to be more honored in the breach than in the observance. The democratic vision, I sincerely believe, was the grandest communal and social ideal ever devised by men. I am referring, however, to men who were, in part, a product of forces typically prevailing in our pre-technological past. That same ideal is also, unfortunately, now somewhat absurd, *but only in relation to the social complexity of our era*. Commitment to it is well intentioned and quite honorable. But if human development in the coming decades is to generate increasing social welfare, the democratic vision, as it has traditionally existed, will have to be bypassed. A premonition of this unhappy eventuality was foreseen by Michael.[17]

To make matters worse, the success of the democratic vision, would not even be guaranteed if all our citizens were thoroughly conversant with the requirements we have already discussed. This is because the social system of a mass society contains so many components, possessing such complex feedback relationships, closed-loop relationships and cross-transpositional influences, as to be very unwieldy and unstable for purposes of management and control. Furthermore, new, exogenous factors are always being brought into play, in a mass society—factors which play havoc with the scientific desideratum of predictability and control. And, of course, among the least controllable of all the exogenous factors that may disequilibrate society conceived of as a "system" in the engineer's sense of this term, are the vagaries of the human mind and heart. Among these vagaries are political caprice, group impulse, mass dissatisfaction accompanied by sabotage or revolution, uninformed self-interest, and the restlessness that derives from excessive social control. All of these may create "system breaks" just as effectively as the introduction of radically new technology.

Then, too, the standard, historical forms of Original Sin are still with us: intellectual laziness, spiritual sloth, and the self-hypnotism incorporated in the absurd, liberal doctrine that unqualifiedly encourages *self-interest*. Intellectual laziness guarantees folly and error in decision-making. Spiritual sloth guarantees political and social alienation in the form of political and social apathy that everyone bewails and to which everyone makes some contribution in one or more of the social aspects of our lives. As for the doctrine of self-interest, that has been encouraged by our anachronistic, liberal heritage, it is, perhaps, the leading roadblock to ethical regeneration and the recapture of the much-needed, religious impulse in the affairs of men. The credo that encourages the quest for self-interest is precisely the monkey-wrench

[17]Donald N. Michael. *Cybernation: The Silent Conquest.* Santa Barbara, California: Center For The Study Of Democratic Institutions, 1962. See in particular the section entitled "After The Take-Over," pp. 44-47.

in our system of social complexity. It is guaranteed to prevent a holistic approach to the social complexity by which we are surrounded. It is also guaranteed to prevent the achievement of general welfare, together with the satisfaction that would derive from such achievement. Equally, it is a credo that encourages us to adopt tunnel vision and local attention and to live in the here and now. The doctrine of self-interest disinclines us to consider the *future* effects of our actions—not only upon others but also upon ourselves. This is one of the more unhealthy components of the democratic vision—a component that does not gear us to ready ourselves for social change.

It is for reasons such as these that the democratic vision is insufficient both for our time and for the emerging future. These reasons apply to every revamped form of democracy currently being proposed just as much as they apply to the traditional Western forms that look to political, democratic stability in terms of the balance among countervailing powers. But, as a matter of fact, most contemporary commitment to democracy is to the countervailing form, and commitment to that form is dedication to a world gone by, the anachronistic pictures of which we foolishly carry around in our heads as though they reflected current realities. Once we decide to slough off those historical features of the democratic credo which are incompatible with the present and the foreseeable future, what remains may still be called "democracy," but it will be only linguistic inertia that prompts us to retain the name. The old, democratic ideals, without drastic revision, constitute a vision that will not keep. Commitment to them becomes a patent absurdity. Drastic revision of the democratic credo is now long overdue.

Assorted Visions and Commitments

The current scene boasts of many new visions. There is a whole spectrum of proposals for the reconstitution and redefinition of democracy, whose advocates may be radical, liberal or conservative in outlook. Many of these proposals are well intentioned, politically knowledgeable and blessed with a sense of *realpolitik*. But in my estimation they must fail for *at least* three reasons. First, they lack detailed blueprints for doing a better job of promoting social welfare than our current, lame, countervailing forms of democracy. Second, they do not really address themselves to the development of new, democratic institutions that are equally adaptable both to technology and to our mass society. Third, their leaders are infected with the *animus dominandi*, that is, the political form of Original Sin, in which the lust for power exceeds the love of principle. Since men are not angels, if any of these proposals ever succeeded politically in establishing a jurisdictional, power base, we would be treated to a Western form of 1984. I suspect that in a matter of years or decades the socially sensitive would soon be overcome with a political feeling of *déjà vu* in which all the ugly, social realities of the present would remain, but baptized with new labels and justified and rationalized with up-to-date forms of Nu-Think and Aesopian language. The justification for this pessimism is that the citizen of the West has been conditioned to deal with a politics of personalities and candidates rather than a politics of issues. While this defect remains in force, no institutional or credal variants of democracy will bring on the good life.

There is also a spectrum concerned with the quest for community. Undergirded by a decentralist rejection of bigness and its accompaniment of alienated forms of bureaucracy, we are witnessing a renascence of the communal spirit. This renascence is taking on many forms, running from homesteading at one extreme, through new types of town planning by Buckminster Fuller, to British and American New Towns, on the other. There are the hundreds of youth communes and homesteading experiments across the country. Some of these are described in the new journal, *The Mother Earth News*.[18] These are the new, ideological experiments in community, one example of which is *Twin Oaks*,[19]

---

[18]*The Mother Earth News* (TMEN), a bi-monthly organ, is published at North Madison, Ohio. Its purposes are best described in the words of its editors. TMEN "is a bimonthly publication edited by, and expressly for, today's influential 'hip' young adults. The creative people. The doers. The ones who make it all happen. Heavy emphasis is placed on alternative life styles, ecology, working with nature and doing more with less."

[19]*Twin Oaks* is published at Louisa, Virginia. Information about this community appears regularly in its mimeographed periodical, *The Leaves Of Twin Oaks*, which began publication in July, 1967. It is established on a farm of 123 acres.

whose members, impressed by Skinner's theories and experimental successes and by his novel, *Walden Two*, seek to put into practice a concrete and current example of a community established on a psychological base. Abroad, we have the establishment of Auroville,[20] near Pondicherry, India. This community, the world's first, planetary city, seeks to realize international brotherhood on the basis of the philosophy and teachings of the Indian sage and philosopher, Sri Aurobindo.[21] Abroad, too, we have the Kibbutz[22] movement in Israel, an important phenomenon in the modern quest for community.

In the US it is the youth commune, however, which is the most important development in the decentralist spectrum. Here again I foresee failure for this new vision of community, for several reasons. 1) Many of these communes are parasitic on their host society, in that they are dependent upon that host society for the very technology they employ. 2) These communes make no provision for meeting community needs for large-scale, producers' goods. 3) A United States of decentralized communes would not last very long, if it could not defend itself, from a takeover by an ideologically, oriented and globally aggressive USSR. Yet communes make no provision for national defense. 4) Most of these communes, unlike Goodman says,[23] are failing to distinguish between functions that need to be centralized on a national scale and functions that need to be decentralized on a community scale. 5) These communes are developing a new form of provincialism—ecological provincialism—in which they do not try to work for a balanced area or regional ecology with other nearby communities.

[20]Auroville, not yet complete, is being built with the help of architects and engineers from various countries. Information on this community is available from its periodical, *Equals One*, which began publication in 1968.

[21]For a brief account of the leading ideas of Sri Aurobindo, see the following: Dilip Kumar Roy. *Among The Great*. Bombay and Calcutta, India: Jaico Publishing House, 1950. See pp. 199-367; for an account of Sri Aurobindo's ideas on the psychology of social development, see the following: Sri Aurobindo. *The Human Cycle*. New York: E.P. Dutton, 1950.

[22]The established and standard work on the kibbutz in Israel is the following: Melford E. Spiro. *Kibbutz: Venture In Utopia*. New York: Schocken Books, 1970. Seventh Printing. 266 pp.

[23]Paul Goodman. *People or Personnel: Decentralizing and the Mixed System*. New York: Random House, 1965.

6) Regional problems of water supply, water pollution and watershed maintenance and regional problems of transportation and communication, are as much a responsibility of our new communes as they are of the rest of us. Nevertheless, no up-to-date revision of the principle of voluntary association, applicable to forms of community federation that are contingent upon joint community problems rather than legally binding for all time, has been worked out by any group of contemporary communes. 7) No real effort is being made by these communes to work out the necessary relationships with the host community within which they are located and whose way of life differs from their own. This "communal isolationism" augurs ill for their future. 8) Almost all of these communes are generationally limited, that is, they are for the young only, and this is probably undesirable for the children who grow up in them.

One could, of course, list many other deficiencies of the commune movement today. One could do likewise for all the other forms of social and political protest we find on the continuum of community decentralization. But that is not the point. What is to the point is the fact that the commune movement is no more geared to the inescapability of social change than the larger society. The communal emphasis on natural food and farming, organic gardening and various other healthy and scientifically sound, agricultural practices, is admirable. But the achievement of a proper relationship with nature and with the soil often seems to result in a quest for a pastoral idyll that would fix the human condition for all time. If successful, communal experimentation is obtainable only at the price of complete secession from the host culture and rejection of the responsibility to participate in the remolding of the larger world nearer to the heart's desire. This can come to no good. It is in these senses that commitment to various, decentralized forms of the dream of community will prove unviable in the long run. The communes are living largely on borrowed capital—tangible and intangible capital that has been accumulated for them by their host society. A dream of reason resting on such questionable, social foundations is a dream that cannot last. A Tolstoian ideal of a return to simplicity, in a world dependent upon ever-changing science and technology, is an ideal that would set the clock back. Such a vision will not keep. Here, too, the quest for community is simply living on borrowed time.

The Agonies and the Ironies of Commitment

To be committed to an objective of which almost everybody approves is to achieve respect and social acclaim. This has been true for hundreds of individuals in the past, such as a Thomas Edison dedicated to applied research, a Sarah Bernhardt dedicated to the theatre and an Albert Schweitzer devoting his life to alleviating the miseries of the African Negro. But authentic commitment to such important and eternal ideals as social truth, brotherhood, freedom and the quest for a just social order often means both suffering, unpopularity, social ostracism and continued misery. This type of commitment also has its heroes but there are far fewer of them than we find engaged in the socially applauded types of commitment. Dedication to ideals which meet the resistance engendered by some of the greatest weaknesses of man—timidity, fear, moral cowardice, herd-mindedness and conformity—is also to risk the hatred and the misunderstanding of the powerful and to precipitate continued abuse at their hands. We have only to think of some of the saints and martyrs of the past who defied the evil propensities of worldly authorities and in our own time of an Alexander Solzhenitsyn or a Martin Luther King. There are and have been, of course, some highly committed souls who have endured suffering and physical privation for clinging to great spiritual and fraternal ideals but who, at the same time, were respected by both friends and enemies. Mahatma Gandhi and Vinoba Bhave in India and the American pacifist, A.J. Muste,[24] come immediately to mind.

Soviet writings give us some idea of the fires of social hell which some of the committed have to endure for years. Solzhenitsyn's three novels, *One Day in the Life of Ivan Denisovich*, *The First Circle* and *Cancer Ward*, are *in part* testimonials to this fact. But for a description of the living hell of daily life in the USSR and the sufferings which had to be borne by outcast in-

[24]For a picture of the ideals and activities to which Muste dedicated himself, see the following volume: Nat Hentoff (ed.). *The Essays Of A.J. Muste*. New York: Simon and Schuster, 1970. 515 pp.

tellectuals who rejected the official hatreds, condemnations and intellectual errors of Soviet officialdom, we have only to read Nadezhda Mandelstam's *Hope Against Hope*.[25] To be spurned by those whose lives you hope to improve, to be informed upon daily so that no one trusts anyone else, to have to acquiesce in official lies and ideological nonsense or risk prison or the firing squad, to observe the limited capacity of most men for social discrimination and perception and the limited achievement of moral autonomy of which they are capable, is to risk losing hope and to turn to stone, psychologically speaking. To witness the evil and cowardice of those who turn in innocence to the authorities, either to save their own skins or to achieve long-term advantages, is to be reminded of how low is the spiritual estate of man. To be victimized, oneself, by the expression of these weaknesses, perpetrated by those whom one wishes to lead towards the light, is to have one's ideals tested by moral fire and to endure the tortures that only the politically depraved harpies of this world can visit upon one. As Mandelstam writes, one notes that corresponding to our own rhetoric of hypocrisy, the Soviets have developed a rhetoric and vocabulary of self-deception, group-think and the rationalization of evil.

But the important consideration in the present connection is not to emphasize the miseries that accompany commitment that runs against the grain of the powers that be. Rather it is to emphasize that the most profound improvements in the human condition, thus far, have been sudden leaps, a sort of social step-function whose high values become conspicuous only at certain times. Revolutionary changes, whether for good or evil, are step-functions in this sense. Human development, though gradual, has for its high points, such step functions, whether they constitute a step backward as with the Nazis or a step forward as in the rise of early Christianity. However—and here is where our emphasis lies—such high points in human development are almost invariably

---

[25]Nadezhda Mandelstam. *Hope Against Hope: A Memoir.* Translated from the Russian by Max Hayward. New York: Atheneum, 1970. This is the book of which Harrison Salisbury has said, "No work on Russia which I have recently read has given me so sensitive and searing an insight into the hellhouse which Russia became under Stalin as this dedicated and brilliant work on the poet Mandelstam by his devoted wife."

the end result of years of commitment by certain individuals to unpopular ideas and ideals. This observation holds just as forcefully for those committed to evil, like Hitler as it does for those who wish to improve the human condition and the lot of the common man. But commitment to the important and timeless ideals of social truth, brotherhood, freedom and the quest for a just, social order must often pay the price in miseries of the type I have already mentioned.

Individuals of the moral stature required for this physically and spiritually abrasive type of commitment are needed more than ever in our overorganized, mass society dominated, as Ellul[26] has emphasized, by the imperatives of technology. But although needed more than ever in a world fast declining morally and socially, such types are becoming more and more rare. The capacity to achieve autonomy in our overorganized and other-oriented society is conspicuous by its absence. The ability to develop workable visions of a social order more utopian in structure than any of the present, more capable of approximating the timeless, universal ideals to which we have already made reference, more egalitarian in scope and ready to take measures to meet the material and spiritual needs of men rather than cater to the adolescent, status and power inequities for which most of them hunger —such ability and such dreams are almost non-existent. The *current* forms of capitalist and socialist thinking and activity do not measure up to these timeless ideals. The traditional, democratic credo is out of kilter with the exigencies and features of the technological age and the overorganized, mass society of the present. Many of the current variations of democracy that are being worked out on paper likewise fail to take stock of the special features of the new world being bequeathed us by emerging science and technology. As for the experiments on the decentralist spectrum, they are almost all politically and culturally secessionist, living only for the present, unaware of the social and political complexities of the age, and unoriented to human groups elsewhere or to coming generations. They stand on the shoulders of giants and, in the realm of political innovation, they give birth to dwarfs. Almost no one cares any more to do the hard thinking re-

[26]Jacques Ellul. *The Technological Society*. Translated from the French by John Wilkinson. New York: Knopf, 1964.

quired to produce new and detailed social visions that will, hopefully, increase the fund of human welfare. Fewer still care to commit themselves to *any* vision—new or old. We thus find ourselves staring at a sinkhole of commitment and while this sinkhole lasts, real changes in the horizons of human development are most unlikely.

We come now to our concluding thoughts on commitment and human development. I have said that in the context of commitment and the visions that underly it, the cardinal error that men make, in the words of Bacon,[27] is to give out "a dream of our own imagination for a pattern of the world." In other words commitment in action to a vision with *fixed*, ideological meaning and a vision which takes little stock of changing circumstances over time, is folly. Yet all our visions are of this nature. They become Procrustean beds into which every social fact must be fitted and into which every unassimilatable idea must be bedded down after proper trimming and verbal distortion of its essence. We are not saying that all visions should be jettisoned. That would be patently absurd. Many are genuinely useful and are closer approximations to social reality than others. But all visions should be modified with time so as to be adapted to the circumstances of every period. An even more drastic consideration is that they should be perennially re-examined to see if, in fact, they *are* relevant to the circumstances and conditions of the age. It would be foolish, however, to treat them as immutable prescriptions for action in a realm of Platonic, pure ideas.

Western man now needs a new type of institution, the *ideological* or *credal review*, the analogue of *judicial review*, whose function it would be to re-examine our social visions against the knowledge of the time and the circumstances of the age. Those who would perform such critical, screening and re-evaluation functions would be the *ombudsmen* of our social visions. The annual, quinquennial or ten-year reports they would deliver, would enable each of us to determine to what visions he could still afford to commit himself and to schedule unselfishly his disposable time to the realization of each of these. This would

[27]Francis Bacon. *The Great Instauration: The Plan of the Work*, 1620. Reprinted in *Selected Writings of Francis Bacon* (with an introduction and notes by Hugh G. Dick). New York: Modern Library, 1955. pp. 439-451.

give us a more sensible and a more rational way of guiding human development. It would ensure our expectations with respect to increased social welfare and deepen our hope for a human condition that can create the maximum good for the greatest number. The inauguration of *ideological review* would reduce the heartaches and frustrations that have traditionally accompanied the exercise of misplaced social and moral idealism. It would give fresh content to the concept of "mutual aid." In the process we would have to learn the truth of the assertion that *we are always at the crossroads of social renewal and that, because this is so, no vision will keep.*

Ideology Versus Scientific Rationality

M ANY ANSWERS are being furnished today, pur-
porting to show how the quest for community may
be realized and how our growing social complexity may be
managed. Most of these answers fall into one of two great
categories. They are either ideological and utopian in
nature or they are practical and experimental. Into the
latter category fall all those answers which depend upon
the following considerations: a restatement of community
purposes, anchored to available resources and human nature as we know it; explicit recognition of those values
which men seek collectively and which are feasible in terms
of the developments and potentialities of modern science
and technology; support of those types of social change
which can be ushered into being by the investigative
methods of modern science and the procedures of rationalization and efficiency which industry and technology have
generated; and a willingness to accomplish all of these
aims without increasing the fund of alienation in our midst.

It therefore behooves us to examine these two broad
categories of response to the task of managing social complexity in our time. In the section which follows we shall
try to deal with the irrelevance and inadequacy of ideology
for this task. In the second section of this paper we shall
try to focus attention upon some of the methods now used
for decision-making—both economic and social decision-
making—in the face of our growing social complexity.
After all, the methods of science and human reason—aided
and abetted by the social and ethical aspects of the religious

THE MIDWEST QUARTERLY, Autumn, 1968,
vol. 10, #1, 25-43.

impulse—are, surely, the only methods which can prove feasible. These are the methods which we will have to fall back upon in generating new communities and in improving existing ones. If they fail, we shall have no answers. But such failure is, of course, unthinkable.

The Irrelevance of Ideology to The Issues of Our Time

The quest for community has been a perennial one for man. This quest intensified when men began to live in cities and to organize their relations on a large geographic scale, either by natural regions or by spatially widespread, political confederations imposed by military rule. When communal life broke down, at any time during the last 8000 years or so, men tried to explain these breakdowns to themselves in terms of such notions as punishment by the gods for their misdeeds, or—in more sophisticated terms—by noting the widespread refusal to live by reason and seek virtue (Socrates), or by lamenting the flagrant violation of the religious impulse and group ethics, or by declaring that moral abandonment of the truths revealed by God (Christianity) was responsible for human tragedy and suffering. As literacy and technology spread, as industrialization and its associated, social stratification took root, the nature of the explanations offered for the failure of community changed. Men now began to develop ideologies instead of religious or philosophical orientations. Ideologies such as anarchism, socialism, communism, democracy, fascism, syndicalism, utopianism, etc., now made their appearance. Citizens who were not politically and communally apathetic began to polarize themselves around conflicting ideologies. A polar ideology which expressed dissatisfaction with the existing social order and which purported to explain its breakdowns would be used to challenge it. An ideology of apology for the existing social order would be used to defend it. Usually the ideology of apology was one which explained communal failures on other grounds than the alleged weaknesses of the system. The breakdowns would be explained by referring to citizen irresponsibility, to the non-cooperation of certain political leaders, etc. These apologia implicitly accepted the existing fabric of society.

Ideologies fail to deal with complete social breakdown or even some of the more limited of society's contingencies, for a variety of reasons. Sometimes they fail because they have been spun originally out of whole cloth, by single minds, trying to operate from personal experience, reading and observation. These latter three avenues for trying to explain society and its breakdowns are insufficient, since they lack the logico-empirical and public controls required by modern social science. No matter how astute the individual theorist and ideologue may be, no single man's experience, reading or observation can be sufficient to understand the "social-go" of things and suggest appropriate remedies for community failures. Karl Marx underemphasized the psychological and social inertia of the farmer and peasant in the traditional society. Owens relied too much on the fund of goodwill among men. Adam Smith thought that *economic man* would continue to be dominant in highly literate societies—like those of the West—and he was greatly mistaken in this assumption. With literacy come knowledge and social imagination and with these come dissatisfactions with the traditional scheme of things and new visions for social reconstruction. The supporters of Fascism—whether of the German, Italian or Japanese variety—prior to World War II, placed far more confidence in the dominance of men's aggressive impulses than a knowledge of the rich fabric of human motivation could justify. The systematizers of Western Christianity— whether St. Thomas Aquinas, Martin Luther, John Calvin, to name but a few—were too parochial in their viewpoints to hit upon a way of life that could be made universal or to discover a set of transcendental convictions which would be well-nigh acceptable everywhere.

Sometimes ideologies fail because they frame and freeze a credo which was socially insightful for a given time and place but which made no provision for drastic changes in the social processes of the system they dealt with and which failed to recognize, in advance, that the patterns of individual human behavior, as they knew them, would not be fixed for all time. These latter types of failure are characteristic of those ideologies—like modern socialism and communism—which do not recognize what the American economist Kenneth Boulding calls a "system break." A "system break" is a concept which refers to the fact that new science and technology or the appearance of very novel social conditions, such as an inadequate resources/population ratio for keeping body and soul together, create an environment or generate an assemblage of social processes and institutions quite different from those prevailing when the ideology was systematically developed. As a result the ideology itself becomes an irrelevant and inadequate form of social therapy for the new conditions, or it may even be dangerous therapy in which the proposed cures are worse than the diseases they were meant to deal with. The degree to which ideologies fail to take stock of changing social conditions in the world today—and what I am about to mention also applies, unfortunately, to the optimists who see no difficulties ahead for modern, Western capitalism—are sometimes quite striking.

Thus, Georg Borgstrom, Professor of Food Science at Michigan State University, USA, recently wrote an important paper relevant to the absurdities of modern ideological expectations and to the extravagances of free-enterprise system theorists. This paper, appearing in *The Centennial Review* (Summer 1967) and entitled "Food—The Great Challenge Of This Crucial Century," soberly dispatches all the current optimism of the West and all the millennial dreams of socialistic and communistic ideologues. It does this by pointing out all the facts—agrobiological, technological, demographic, nutritional, medical, economic, geographic, sociological—which would make the expectations of ideologues concerning man's immediate future hilarious if they were not so tragic. Borgstrom has tried to make leftist ideologues and Western optimists face the stark tragedy which current limitations upon the world's resources are creating for all of mankind's legitimate, but currently unrealizable, dreams. The optimism which he is so bitterly attacking can best be reflected, I think, in the following congeries of predictions, drawn from the statements of many different Russian and American scientists, whose ignorance of social possibilities and problems stands in marked contrast to their professional and technical erudition and their personal hopes. Among the recent predictions made by these scientists are the following: By the year 2000 voyages to the moon will be commonplace; so will inhabited artificial satellites. All food will be completely synthetic. Agriculture and fisheries will have become superfluous. The world's population will have increased fourfold but will have stabilized. Sea water and ordinary rocks will yield all the necessary metals. Disease, as well as famine, will have been eliminated; and there will be universal hygienic inspection and control. The problems of energy production will have been completely resolved.

Sometimes an ideology is an outright form of mythmaking, cynically employed by its users to galvanize political support and to achieve numerical strength, but otherwise useless as social theory. This, of course, was the case for the theoretical basis—such as it had—of Nazism or of the doctrines developed to support Mussolini's corporate state. Sometimes an ideology is a product of what logicians call "black and white thinking," that is, of the tendency to polarize explanations of social breakdowns in terms of good and evil—the oldest drama known to man and the simplest to comprehend. Under the aegis of polarized thinking, Christianity sees human suffering and its amelioration in terms of God and the Devil, and Zoroastrianism sees it in essentially the same terms—a conflict between Ahriman and Ahura Mazda, the forces of darkness and light, respectively.

Modern man transforms this primal theme somewhat, because of a greater intellectual sophistication, but he still preserves the dualism of explanation. And so for the late 19th century ideologue and the 20th century doctrinaire, social breakdowns are to be explained in terms of a conflict between communism and capitalism—a conflict which receives domestic expression in various forms and in various struggles on the international scene. This polarization is sometimes expressed in a variant of the preceding dichotomy—the managers and the workers, the bourgeoisie and the proletariat, the haves and the have-nots, the advanced (exploiting) and the colonial (exploited) countries, the industrial exploiters and the industrially oppressed—and, indeed, in many other similar antinomies. All of these polarizations are essentially myths—containing some truth to be sure—but whatever truth ideologies possess, they are stretched, as in Procrustean beds, to fit aspects of social reality for which they were never intended. Often this stretching is absurd because of "system breaks" which have occurred and which have produced conditions that never existed at the time the polarizations in question were originally and systematically formulated.

In addition to the broad, universalizing failures of ideologies, they also fail because of specific beliefs that will not pass the test of human experience. Thus in some forms of Marxist theory, art is regarded as social in its genesis and is seen as a reflection of human suffering and frustration, as these are produced by morally evil, social stratification and exploitation. Ideologues who hold to such a belief seriously will then argue that art will disappear in the classless society. But anyone familiar with *The Social History of Art,* the four-volume work of that great art historian, Arnold Hauser, will have little difficulty in recognizing the social absurdity of this doctrinaire, aesthetic credo. Democracy, too, has its specific ideological content—content which ignores the demands of fact and scientific confirmation. Thus, democracy assumes that the average voter is in a position to understand the problems of his community and possesses the wherewithal to pass judgment on various proposed solutions for these problems. This, of course, is empirically a myth which is vitally necessary to sustain democracy, and the degree to which it is a myth is splendidly set forth in such a book as Ferdinand Lundberg's *The Treason of the People.* Still another current myth of the democratic West is that its technology and its abundance are the fruits of both democratic processes and democratic institutions. Clearly this belief is absurd and ignores social reality. German Fascism was equally able to advance technology and create abundance. Russian communism has also been able to advance scientifically and technologically and has also raised the standard of living of its people. It may have done so far too slowly to impress the supporters of Western type democracy—but the inferior level of Soviet technology and Soviet consumption standards can be explained on social and scientific grounds which are quite neutral towards the merits or undesirability of the Soviet socio-political system. Considerations such as these indicate clearly enough, I believe, that science and technology are ideologically neutral and that any form of government may be able to exploit them in an economic—not a communally—satisfactory way.

Ideologies, then, are myths which serve to galvanize human support and human action. They are not intended to be taken seriously as theoretical explanations of social breakdowns or as recipes for the solution of our social ills. One sees this deficiency of the ideological mentality beautifully illustrated in such a book as *Ideologies in World Affairs,* written by Andrew Gyorgy and George D. Blackwood. Ideologies may suggest ideal modes of social reconstruction, to the extent that they possess Utopian elements, but they furnish no methods, no plans and no blueprints for detailed social reconstruction—a fact which becomes strikingly clear when one reads such a volume as Karl Mannheim's *Ideology And Utopia.* One can always describe a finished Utopia on paper. If asked how to achieve that Utopia, however, we embark upon another set of intellectual considerations entirely. The dominant barrier to social reconstruction in the twentieth century is its social complexity—a characteristic which bids fair to increase with the passage of time. Ideologies cannot deal with this social complexity because ideologues are more concerned with how to get power rather than with how to solve the community's problems.

Are there, then, recipes in the world today for dealing with the problems of the modern community—recipes which recognize the existence of social complexity and which try to deal with it head-on? The answer is that there are many such recipes today and that more and more new methods are constantly being developed for dealing with the social complexities of our time. These are really—when you get down to it—the social complexities of an age of science and technology. These methods are both anti-ideological and non-ideological in nature and they are antipathetic to every type of doctrinaire posture. They are also methods which are very technical in nature. They are technical in the sense that they are usually quantitative in their procedures. But they have one thing in common. Their thrust is towards the solution of a problem. By contrast an ideology tries to account—usually inadequately—for the genesis of a problem and tries to convince its prospective adherents that if they turned out the present holders of power and replaced them with certain new seekers of the same power, all will be well, community breakdowns will be remedied and the community will prosper. In an ideologically oriented society men are permitted to act rationally in science and economics, while giving lip-service to the prevailing ideology. Their actions, however, need bear little relationship, if any, to their ideological orientation. Russian biologists may apply genetics to agricultural problems of the USSR—as they did in the Stalin era—and verbally march to the doctrinaire tunes played by the ideologically oriented Russian "biologist," Lysenko. And Red Chinese nuclear specialists may send up successfully a fresh variant of a nuclear bomb, while chanting passages at the same time from the sacred writings of Mao Tse-Tung.

The newer methods for dealing with social problems and social complexity are—unlike modern ideologies— down to earth. They are concerned with increasing the amount of social welfare in our midst. They make the community's problems explicit and they define them very carefully. They take stock of the resources available to solve those problems. They note and try to work around existing difficulties and political barriers to various types of proposed solution. This is done by means of what Alvin Weinberg has called "A Technological Fix." Those who practise these methods are refining them all the time, by means of what has come to be called PERT (*Program Evaluation And Review Technique*). Above all, the practitioners of the newer methods adapt them to changing circumstances, changing social and material resources and changing political feasibilities and realities. In this sense their practitioners not only recognize the importance of system breaks in creating social complexity but they also recognize with Aristotle that "politics is the art of the possible." It is then of vital importance that we become acquainted with some of these newer methods to which we have been referring. We shall deal with these in the section which follows, the second and last of this paper.

Scientific Rationality and Our Social Problems

In the preceding section of this paper we emphasized the irrelevance of the ideological approach for the task of achieving *The Great Society*. Instead, we asserted, what is needed is a set of scientific and rational techniques— married to a sense of social value and an enlightened public philosophy—for dealing with the social problems which have been generated by the increasing social complexity of our age. We reserved the task of briefly describing the nature of such recently developed techniques for the final section of this paper. We, therefore, propose below merely to characterize as briefly as possible *some* of the newer methods for dealing with those of our social problems which have become anchored in the increasing social complexity of our age. Among the many new methods for dealing with social complexity which have been developed in recent years are the following: the use of cost-benefit ratio analysis, operations research, general systems theory, linear and dynamic programming, input-output analysis, methods for the allocation of scarce resources (allocation theory), decision-theory, game theory, information theory, and many others. Each of these methods is highly technical and both the expository exigencies of the subject matter as well as limitations of space would make extended treatment here inappropriate. If we can suggest, however, what each of the first two methods is and what each can do, something will have been accomplished towards the amplification of our theme.

The Use of Cost-Benefit Ratios. This is a method which is used in national budgeting for given objectives. Suppose a governmental agency wishes to achieve a given objective, such as flood control, the eradication of a given disease, or an increase in the numbers of those employed in a given area. Consider the latter objective. Let us say five different measures are proposed to increase area employment. Those who employ cost benefit analysis will then reach some sort of agreement on the *benefits* to be derived from increased employment in the given area. These benefits will, of course, vary somewhat from one to another of the five different measures which have been proposed. These will be such benefits as reduced government welfare payments, more Federal taxes made available, more spending and therefore more business volume, more use of fixed burden in factories, more training of prospective employees in marketable skills, less sickness, more available education to the offspring of the unemployed, etc. Where possible, all these benefits are expressed in monetary terms, being regarded as wealth or increased income produced, or as dollars of Federal expenditures saved, or as an amount of future increase in wage potentials. There are innumerable ways of categorizing benefits and, in our example, we have mentioned only a very few of them.

These estimated benefits are then expressed in dollars for a short and finite period, say a five-year span. Then an estimate is made of the costs of each of the five measures over the same period. Finally, for each measure, total benefits over the period are divided by total costs over the same period. This gives us the cost-benefit ratio (CBR). If the CBR is less than 1, the measure is clearly undesirable, for it would then be better and more generous to give the money involved in the prospective costs to the unemployed. The share per capita of income thus achieved would be better for those who were recently without any income than that resulting from the prospective benefits of the

75

measure in question. If the CBR equals 1, then there would, in fact, be no gain. The measure which resulted in a CBR of 1 would simply be a device for transferring income from employed taxpayers to hitherto unemployed citizens. It would have the advantage, however, of enabling the recipients to maintain their self-respect because their new income would not have the appearance of being a welfare payment, since services would have been provided in order to earn it. This same measure would also have a certain disadvantage. The costs applied—to be sure— would produce benefits of the same financial magnitude, but the time lag in gaining these benefits would be greater than that involved in disbursing the same amount of funds directly to the unemployed. If the CBR is greater than 1, then the measure is clearly desirable. Furthermore, if for all five of our hypothetical measures, the CBR had been unequal in value, then, in general, the best measure to use to decrease unemployment in a given area would be that measure which yielded the highest value for the CBR.

Obviously the CBR is a payoff ratio. It is also a measure of decision-making efficiency. It asks that social returns per dollar expended be greater than each dollar of cost itself. The use of the CBR makes it possible to wind one's way through various aspects of existing social complexity, even where one does not have an understanding of the genesis of that complexity itself. One deals with it without necessarily being able to control it. One produces social welfare that is immediately felt by its recipients without a priori, ideological arguments to the effect that if such and such is done the social fabric will be improved and economic suffering reduced. Furthermore, one does not have to guess which of several measures will be optimal. Where both costs and benefits are chiefly pecuniary in nature—although this need not always be the case—the feasibility of the various measures can be expressed in a common, monetary unit and, in this way, an operational definition of "best measure" is immediately applicable. The CBR is the basic method employed in the United States in what has come to be known as the Planning-Programming-Budgeting System (PPBS).

Operations Research. Operations research can be regarded, in the broadest sense, as the application of scientific method to any type of complex, large-scale practical problem. Usually such an application becomes transformed into the understanding and control of large-scale complex systems. These systems may occur in the control of production and distribution in private industry or they may involve the growing, gathering and processing of produce in agriculture. They may involve planning for an entire industry or for an entire government. Essentially the operations research analyst faces complexity of some sort—industrial, military, social or economic. When he faces the social complexity of the responsibilities inherent in a modern, large-scale, national government, we then have the typical situation for which the ideological mentality would be completely irrelevant.

The field of operational research depends on the interpretation of the word "operations" in the definition. In war, operational research was applied to the use of weapons, to tactics, and to strategy. In the peacetime application of operational research, studies are directed, for example, to the use of equipment and manpower, to operating procedures, and to the solution of those many problems faced by management in controlling or operating factories or public utilities, or by Government authorities in planning. In the broadest sense, then, we may say that operations research is the application of the scientific method to the study of the operations of large complex organizations or activities. Its objective is to provide top-level administrators with a quantitative basis for decisions that will increase the effectiveness of such organizations in carrying out their basic purposes. Thus, although the activity consists of research, it is reasearch with a severely practical goal. But no brief definition, of course, can be expected to convey more than a vague notion of operations research, its subject matter, its methods, its distinguishing characteristics, its significance.

Our interest in this second section, of course, is in operations research applied to the socially complex problems of government, where—in terms of the points emphasized in our first section—an ideological approach would be simply irrelevant and inappropriate. When, however, the socially complex problems facing modern governments are dealt with by the operations research practitioner, they are handled by methods and procedures which are no different from the methods and procedures employed in controlling large-scale systems in war, industrial management, large-scale farming, etc. For this reason we shall mention here the board-gauge methods of operations research, as they are used in industry, since, as we have just remarked, these methods do not differ from one context to another and are therefore also employed in governmental decision-making. The following, then, are the major phases of an operations research project or an operations research attack upon a national problem of a socially complex nature.

First, the problem has to be formulated clearly. This means that in the system under study, one has to know what the social benefits and the social disadvantages are and who receive these benefits and who suffer these disadvantages. Then one has to ascertain who controls the system under analysis, and whether that control is total and understood, partial and understood, total and yet not comprehended, partial as well as not comprehended, deliberate or inadvertent, continuous or intermittent, structurally modifiable or structurally inelastic, and many similar considerations. Where control is deliberate, the objectives of the controllers of the system must be known and understood, although, of course, they need not be sympathetically shared. Then, too, the constraints upon the system must be understood, that is to say, the alternative ways in which it can function must be known and the various alternative courses of action not permitted by the system, must also be known.

Once the problem within the system has been clearly formulated, the operations research analyst tries to construct a mathematical model to represent the system with which he has to deal. This is the second but, perhaps, the most basic step. The reason this is so is that the adequacy and reality of the model which has been developed will determine the quality of the solution which is eventually proposed. Deriving a solution from the model in question is the operations research analyst's third step. The quality and adequacy of that solution, however, will be determined by the fourth step. In this step the researcher or policymaker makes certain predictions concerning the behavior of the system and he makes these from the model he has developed. The adequacy of these predictions can then be tested by seeing either how well the mathematical model would have postdicted the known, previous states of the system or how well it will predict the future states of the system. In either case one must know what one means by valid data for testing and must know where to get such data.

The fifth step depends on what we have already described in the first section of this paper as a "system break." In this step we wish to establish controls over the solution. The mathematical model used as a solution for the social or economic problem which was originally the focus of attention assumed certain factors as dependent and certain other factors as independent. When the national system being studied changes drastically over time, because of such factors as new developments in science and technology, new population pressures, drastic and fundamental changes in the attitudes and social psychology of the population involved, basic changes in the savings and/or consumption patterns of the population, and in similar ways, then we clearly have a "system break." At this point the mathematical model originally developed can no longer be used. It must now either be modified to reflect the "new system" which is the "old system" after the latter has experienced a "system break" or—if this is impossible—an entirely new mathematical model must be developed to deal with the same class of problems and phenomena. In establishing controls over a solution, one must develop tools for determining when significant changes have occurred and, in addition, one must establish rules for modifying our original solutions if, in fact, system breaks have occurred.

In all of the preceding methods for dealing with contemporary problems in a socially complex milieu, we have said nothing about a very important matter. All of the newer methods for dealing with our problems tend to define welfare in terms of the *quantity* of goods and services which a modern economy seeks to provide for its citizens. But most of the practitioners of the newer methods say nothing about the *"quality* of life" which is produced by a society which is bending all its efforts to increase the *amount* of welfare to be made available to its citizens. Are there any thinkers in the West today who are concerned with the "quality of welfare"? The answer is, of course, in the affirmative.

Today there is a movement—a minority one to be sure —in the United States, led by thinkers who now declare that it is not sufficient if we rest content only with the successful management of our social complexity. It is important, assert these thinkers, to make certain that, in solving the problems created by that social complexity, we ensure that the quality of life which results from the solutions instituted meets genuine human needs and strivings.

80

The human needs and strivings referred to are on the psychological, cultural, intellectual, aesthetic, social, political, educational, ethical and religious planes. These thinkers demand that a wise consensus be reached with respect to social goals and national purposes. They demand, in addition, that "social indicators" be developed which shall be measures of the degree to which *the non-material goals* of contemporary man, are being fulfilled. They call for a new type of statistics—"quality-welfare statistics"—which shall consist of data that reflect the improvement or deterioration in the quality of our national, social life. These social indicators should enable us to assess where we stand and are going with respect to our values and goals, and to evaluate specific programs and determine their impact. The indicators which are needed, according to the thinkers who are on the frontiers of research in this new area, will require an abandonment of the Ptolemaic perspective with which people see the world revolving around themselves and require instead a kind of Copernican revolution through which we may better regard our decisions as involving the total social system, and not only that part of it which revolves around our own persons.

A leading work in connection with this new field—concerned with the measurement of the degree to which desirable social goals are being achieved and concerned with a quantitative representation of the quality of our social life—is a book which bears the title *Social Indicators,* edited by Raymond A. Bauer. This is a book which can be compared with the efforts of the economists thirty years ago to create a stable and useful set of economic indicators. But the problem with economic indicators is that they deal not with "how good" but with "how much"; not with the quality of our lives but rather with the quantity of goods and dollars. True social indicators can function as a guide for economic indicators. Clearly, the implications of the development of social indicators are revolutionary.

Current work being done on social indicators is meant to challenge the existing framework of statistics used as guides for governmental policy-formation and economic decision-making. Bauer's book was under study by certain groups in the United States, the United Kingdom and Canada even before it was published. It is a book which is noteworthy in that it provides the basis for a new type of social accounting—a type that is more likely to reveal the quality of national life than do the present types of economic and social statistics which most governments conventionally employ. The work of these new pioneers in the development of social indicators has, in fact, already been brought to public attention in that well-known American organ of liberal and democratic opinion, *The New Republic*. This was done in an excellently written article entitled "The Future-Planners" (February 25, 1967) by Andrew Kopkind.

The importance of the development and of the use of social indicators is this: The technical methods for the management of our social complexity and for the solution of those of our contemporary problems embedded in that complexity can be used to restrict our solutions only to those which improve the quality of our national life. If this is done—and only if this is done—can we then say that economic and social decision-making have reached maturity. If this is done—and only if this is done—can we then say that we have begun to solve the most pressing domestic problems of our time. And finally—if the solutions to our problems conform also to the demand that the quality of our lives be improved at the same time— then we shall really be able to say that we are truly succeeding in managing the social complexity of our age. If we can do this, then, indeed, we shall also be able to say that we are moving towards the establishment of the Great Society. Can we ask for more?

SELECTED BIBLIOGRAPHY

American Management Association, *Operations Research: Explained and Applied* (New York: American Management Association, 1956).

Raymond A. Bauer, editor, *Social Indicators* (Cambridge, Massachusetts: The M. I. T. Press, 1966).

Georg Borgstrom, "Food—The Great Challenge Of This Crucial Century" (*The Centennial Review*, Vol. 11, No. 3, Summer 1967).

Kenneth Boulding, *The Meaning Of The 20th Century. The Great Transition* (New York: Harper, 1964).

Edward C. Bursk and John F. Chapman, editors, *New Decision-Making Tools For Managers* (New York: Mentor Books, 1965). See particularly Robert H. Miller, "How To Plan And Control With Pert," chapter 3.

C. West Churchman et al., *Introduction to Operations Research* (New York: Wiley, 1957).

Daedalus, Utopia (Vol. 94, No. 2, Spring 1965).

Elizabeth B. Drew, "HEW grapples with PPBS" (*The Public Interest*, No. 8, Summer, 1967).

Andrew Gyorgy and George D. Blackwood, *Ideologies In World Affairs* (Waltham, Massachusetts: Blaisdell, 1967).

Arnold Hauser, *The Social History Of Art*, 4 vols. (New York: Vintage Books, 1963).

Erich Jantsch, *Technological Forecasting In Perspective* (Paris: Organisation For Economic Co-operation And Development, 1967). See particularly the section entitled "Economic Analysis," 190-200 in Part II, "Techniques Related To Technological Forecasting."

Andrew Kopkind, "The Future-Planners" (*The New Republic*, Vol. 156, No. 8, Issue 2726, February 25, 1967).

Ferdinand Lundberg, *The Treason Of The People* (New York: Harper, 1954).

Karl Mannheim, *Ideology And Utopia. An Introduction To The Sociology Of Knowledge* (New York: Harcourt, Brace, 1936).

Glenn Negley and J. Max Patrick, editors, *The Quest For Utopia. An Anthology Of Imaginary Societies* (New York: Doubleday, 1962).

Alvin Weinberg, "Can Technology Replace 'Social Engineering'" (*Air Force and Space Digest*, Vol. 50, No. 12, January 1967).

THE FERTILITY OF EXISTENTIAL PERSPECTIVES FOR HISTORICAL ANALYSIS

HISTORY AND THE MORAL POSTURE

IF the purpose of history is not merely to unfold a chronological panorama of the past but also to impose meaning on that panorama for men in the present, then clearly the most important of all the categories of meaning with which the historian should be concerned is the moral significance of past events. But in order to maintain an unambiguous posture towards the moral significance of the historical episode, anyone—historians or otherwise—must have some clear-cut notions of what constitutes the good life. These notions will have relevance to two basic sources of historical action : the individual and the group. If, then, the historian assumes what Mumford[1] christens "axial consciousness", that is to say, a sensitivity towards the relationship between historical events and sought values, he cannot escape the task of passing judgment on historical movements which seem to support some given value-credo, that is to say, some given pattern of the good life, which to him seems desirable or dysgenic. Since the conviction that man can operate along *a moral dimension* is to assume that *man makes himself*, a perspective emphasized, for instance, by such dissimilar types of thinkers as contemporary existentialists and conservative theologians, the historian must pass moral judgment on the trends of his times.

These judgments must be, of course, a type of moral accounting. By this we mean that human decision-making, whether individual or collective, creates either assets or

---

1 Lewis Mumford. *The Transformations of Man.* New York : Collier Books, 1962. 188 pp.

THE VISVA-BHARATI QUARTERLY, 1967-78, vol. 33, #1&2, 62-85.

liabilities in relation to the value-objectives which, to the historian, spell out his notions of what constitutes the good life. The historian's judgments are, therefore, explicitly or implicitly pleas to accentuate some trends or to curtail or reverse others. His is a self-conscious partisanship in that he makes unambiguous the moral bases of his judgments and interpretations. He relates these to the inner meaning of the events he deals with but *he does not inject* these same judgments into those events as part of their characteristics. This would be equivalent to seeing some of these events as events in which the human actors were concerned with moral decisions. At times, this is the case. Most frequently, however, the goals of the actors are ambiguous to themselves and they have not examined too closely the potential consequences of their own actions. When this is the case, the historian must, of course, avoid crediting the actors with a moral context of which they, themselves, are unaware. To impute such a moral dynamism to the actors involved would constitute a historical form of the *pathetic fallacy*.

On those occasions, however, when large groups of men do crystallize some moral decisions over the course of time and these decisions have had, or may have, a serious impact upon the society of which they are a part, then the execution of the historian's moral stance becomes doubly difficult. This is because the moral decisions of others are being weighed in the balance of one's own moral commitments. The tendency for the two different sets of decision-making contexts—those of the historical actors being described and those of the historian, himself—to fuse, to be substituted for one another, is increased. So, too, is the historian's tendency to neglect the task of relating the moral outlook of the actors to the conditions and contingencies of their own time. Instead, he may lapse unwittingly into the habit of relating the actions of historical personages to the "superior," more sophisticated and chronologically later, moral posture of the historian, himself. Sometimes the historian may overlook the task of relating his own value-credo to the conditions and contingencies of his own day. He is especially susceptible to this latter weakness because of the tendency of most men to view their notions of the good life *sub specie aeternitatis* rather than to recognize the great likelihood that the viewpoint adopted may, itself, be a historical *res accidens*. Where the latter is the case the whole context of judgment, which should be, to some extent, relativistic, is being overlooked and, what is worse, there is no basis in such a case for the *axial legitimation* of the historian's point of view.

In invoking a moral fulcrum for the interpretation of history, the historian has to recognize, I believe, that he is adopting a point of view in the realm of scholarship, research and learning, which is against the grain of current, academic fashion. The methods and thoughtways of science are now dominant in the world of learning. The central *motif* in this dominance is "objectivity" and the expression of this objectivity demands that considerations of human value be shunned like the plague. The task of the scholar, it is held, is straightforward description and the search for laws, regularities and patterns underlying aggregate, human behavior. The extreme form of this point of view in the social sciences is, of course, "scientism." The historian who adopts the moral posture as a professional necessity, has to realize that he courts methodological criticism and professional unpopularity—at least from other areas of the social sciences—and that the outcome of his work, when it reflects a moral posture, will be consistently questioned and often rejected precisely because of existing professional emphases and expectations. If he bends to current methodological emphases he must then either assume the role of a cataloguer of events or that of a researcher looking for horizontal or longitudinal patterns among these same events. He is then in no position to give advice or to plead for social redirection—not, at least, in a professional capacity. He can neither a Pangloss nor a Cassandra be. He becomes only a footman to time and in this capacity the existentialist esprit can become no part of his activities or his outlook. In that case his voice is almost wholly lost.

If the historian assumes a moral posture—whether of the existentialist variety or not—he has to be a critic of the presuppositions of his culture. Neutrality, in the form of exposition and description, would make no sense. Guided social change is either in the direction of the historian's notion of the good life or it is undermining that notion. Such change will therefore be evaluated positively or negatively. As an example of the historian's challenge to the presuppositions of his culture, we can cite Baritz's[2] study and critique of the values and assumptions underlying the application of the social sciences to American business and industry. A second example of what we have in mind is Hofstadter's[3] candid and challenging presentation of continued anti-intellectualism in the United States. By the same token the historian can also view his total culture critically and, if that culture is morally provincial, this can be brought out by contrast with larger visions of a human community—visions of a possibility for world-order as contrasted with national outlooks. Wagar's[4] work is case in point. Muck-raking is a kind of

---

2 Loren Baritz. *The Servants of Power*. A History Of The Use Of Social Science in American Industry. Middletown, Connecticut : Wesleyan University Press, 1960. 273 pp.

3 Richard Hofstadter. *Anti-intellectualism in American Life*. New York : Alfred A. Knopf, 1963. 434 pp.

4 W. Warren Wagar. *The City of Man*. Prophecies of a World Civilization in Twentieth-Century Thought. Boston : Houghton Mifflin, 1963. 310 pp.

moral posture but it represents a type of negative morality—negative in the sense that the muckraker deals with the violation of society's ethics and expectations,—but rarely does muckraking reflect the exposer's positive notions of the good life. As an institution, however, muckraking is more the product of journalist's art than the historian's. For this reason we shall say no more about it.

The historian with an existentialist bias must ever alert himself to current trends which have occurred previously and which, in the past, eventuated in aggregate consequences deplored by most social groups. An existentialist posture sensitizes the historian to the possibility that history may repeat itself. To such a historian Original Sin is ever present and the conditions for the germination of evil repeat themselves. In history, as the Church puts it, men rarely avoid the occasion of sin. The worst human passions receive expression again and again, given certain social forces and struggles for power. The historian sensitized to the contemporary form of such considerations will occasionally also project their consequences into the future, in which case he may become a perceptive prophet of gloom, if not of doom, like Burckhardt.[5] Or, on the contrary, while recognizing the possibilities for global disaster if mankind takes the wrong turning, he may be an optimist who sees future trends as leading to an excellence in the human condition, incomparably superior to anything that man has known before. A point of view of this sort characterizes the historically minded philosopher, such as Mora.[6] The proclivity for pessimism towards the future can also be seen in the work

---

5 Jacob Burckhardt. *Force and Freedom.* An interpretation of history. New York : Meridian Books, 1955. 346 pp.

6 Jose Ferrater Mora. *Man At The Crossroads.* Boston : Beacon Press, 1957. 253 pp.

of a theologian with a strong sense of history, such as Niebuhr,[7] or in the humanist-philosopher, Marcel,[8] who possessed the additional virtue of trying to dissipate the moral alienation of our time by translating some of the abstract, philosophical considerations of existentialism into the flesh-and-blood impact of more than twenty dramas.

The historian who finds the existentialist outlook congenial will naturally be a figure who, though he takes cognizance of the sweep and potency of aggregate social forces and though he recognizes the propaedeutic value of large-scale, historical abstractions, yet manages to balance these with a strong feeling for the role of the individual in history. It would make no sense to maintain an existentialist posture and yet see the drama of historical change as due solely to impersonal forces over which men have no control. Where a moral bias exists that inclines the historian to try to remould this world a little nearer to the heart's desire, it would be pointless to believe strongly that men are but particles blown about by cosmic winds. A historian whose viewpoint is strongly tinged with the conviction that the individual may be responsible for significant, historical changes will not be too easily convinced by the de-emphasis of the individual's role in history, as we find it, for example, in Hook.[9] He is likely to be more sympathetic to an *emphasis* on the role of the individual in history, as we find it,

---

7   I am referring here to such works of Niebuhr's as the following : (1) *The Nature And Destiny Of Man.*   New York : Charles Scribner's Sons, 1964.   2 vols. Vol. I, 305 pp, Vol. II, 328 pp. ; (2) *The Irony Of American History.*   New York : Charles Scribner's Sons, 1952, 174 pp. ; and (3) *Moral Man And Immoral Society* : A Study in Ethics and Politics. New York : Charles Scribner's Sons, 1960. 284 pp.

8   Gabriel Marcel.   *Men Against Humanity.*   London : The Harvill Press Ltd.. 1952. 205 pp.

9   Sidney Hook.   *The Hero In History.*   New York : Humanities Press, 1950. 273 pp.

instead, in Plutarch[10] or Huizinga.[11]   To lapse into the abstract attitude in which the drama of history is seen deterministically as the product of social and economic forces which lie outside of men, themselves, would be the opposite of an existentialist *elan*.   The adoption of the latter framework will surely prompt the historian to pay his respects to the balance between large-scale forces of social systems, that carry their own imperatives, but will prompt the historian even more to recognize that these systems and their imperatives can be changed at will through the strength of character, the projective imagination, the social altruism and the moral determination of individual men.

If history is to be more than impersonal description then the historian surely has to have a feeling for the emotional impacts produced by social change.   To be deeply touched by the tragic sense of life is it would seem an inescapable need for a historian with an existentialist outlook.   This, in turn should be accompanied by an awareness of the errors into which individuals and groups have been drawn by pressures whose consequences they ill foresaw.   *Professional* expectations concerning the requirement that he do not tamper with "objective" facts, make it necessary that the historian be detached from his subject, but as *man* and *interpreter* he is free to *become involved* with it.   Only the literary figure — in novels, plays, poems, essays and biographies—is free to show strong feelings about the historical characters and events he describes and to take a certain amount of liberty with historic fact, if this will help to serve the purpose of catharsis so as to move the reader, auditor or viewer.   But although the professional historian cannot take sides in the sense of biasing the facts, he is free to load them with value-

---

10   *Plutarch's Lives.* (Grace Curl, Editor), New York : D. C. Heath And Company, 1957. 376 pp.

11   Johan Huizinga. *Men And Ideas.* History, The Middle Ages, The Renaissance. New York : Meridian Books, Third printing, 1965. 378 pp.

significance by experimenting with styles and treatments that convert what would otherwise be abstract, historical description into discussions which make past events come alive and personalities seem vivid. This is his "existentialist option."

The value inherent in the exercise of this option lies in the fact that past historical events may appear to have some cogency for the life of the reader and seem real to the extent that they reflect the same qualites that he experiences in the life around him. In order to achieve such effects the historian does not have to mix fancy with fact. He does, however, have to present the facts selected and organized for their saliency to the themes of significance with which he is trying to deal so that they absorb the reader as completely — if not more so — than a powerful novel. This must, of course, be accomplished without the use of the *same* artifices, conceits and devices we find in literature and the humanities. Unfortunately, few historians experiment with the *concretization* and *vitalization* of historical writing, in this sense. Gibbons,[12] of course, is an example of one distinguished success along these lines, Burckhardt[13] another. Recent examples of historical writing executed with a humanistic touch, and which at the same time do no violence to the climaxes of historical experience may be seen in the work of a professor of English, turned historian. I refer to the writings of Muller.[14],[15]

12 Edward Gibbon. *The Decline And Fall Of The Roman Empire.* (David Low, Editor). London : Chatto & Windus, 1960. 924 pp.

13 Jacob Burckhardt. *The Age Of Constantine The Great.* New York : Doubleday, 1956. 386 pp.

14 Herbert J. Muller. *The Uses Of The Past.* New York : A Mentor Book, 1954. 384 pp.

15 Herbert J. Muller. *The Loom Of History.* New York : A Mentor Book, 1961. 495 p.

Although the historian cannot afford to rewrite history in an existentialist vein he can allow himself the privilege of trying to understand historical personalities in terms of some of the main features of an existentialist outlook. The network of concepts[16] which characterize the concerns of the existentialist posture—concepts which have been dealt with extensively by Wild[17] and defined by Winn[18]—can certainly *colour* the perspective underlying the historian's interpretation, thus influencing the angle from which historical events and personages may be viewed. Even more important, the interpretation of contemporary trends and forces, the evaluative stand the historian can take towards contempory forms of polar, ideological conflict, the moral bias in assessing the consequences of national and international decisions and the adequacy or obstructiveness of existing institutions to meet human needs— all these can be illuminated by the outlook of existentialsm. But this is not all. The critical judgment rendered on the themes by which one's contemporaries live today and propose to live tomorrow, the examination of the motives underlying group action both intranationally and internationally, and the calling into account the decisions of major leaders who are influencing world-events—these are all matters in the treatment of which an existentialist posture can fund meaning and provide significant insight.

---

16 A tiny sample of the concepts I have in mind would be the following : authenticity, encounter, care, commitment, engagement, bad faith, essence versus existence, anguish, Being and Nothingness, Mitwelt, Umwelt, Eigenwelt, I-It and I and Thou, possibility, responsibility, subjectivity, self-actualization, self-transcendence, subject-object, understanding, value, autonomy, creativity, identity, psychological health and normal growth. Many other existentialist concepts of equal importance have not been mentioned.

17 John Wild. *The Challenge of Existentialism*. Bloomington : Indiana University Press. 1959. 297 pp.

18 Ralph B. Winn. *A Concise Dictionary Of Existentialism*. New York : Philosophical Library. 1960. 122 pp.

In addition, the analysis of ends and means in proposals for social reconstruction, the indictment of mores and measures that treat whole populations as objects rather than human beings and the tendency for politicians and statesmen to get lost in abstractions and administrative procedures and overlook the concrete effects of their actions, are all matters which can be dealt with by the cutting edge of an existentialist position. Finally, the assessment of the quality of life led by his contemporaries, the depiction of the social consequences entailed in the conflicting ideologies of contemporary life, the exposure and indictment of the gap between the values expressed by historical personalities and the moves they make which contradict their expressed values or simply and deliberately fail to support them—all these matters, too, can be treated so as to reflect the existentialist awareness, concern and perspective of the historian familiar with the viewpoints reflected in modern existentialist thought.

There is a second area in which it behooves the historian to move *intellectually*. I am referring to the field of *philosophical anthropology* which can be defined as an *interdisciplinary area* that is concerned, in the widest sense, with the nature of man. Certainly historical analysis in depth has everything to gain in understanding the motives which move men, whether social, psychological or biological. Historical analysis can profit considerably from a knowledge of group dynamics and class motivations, both of which, in part, have been the focus of Mannheim's[19], [20], [21] concern in developing a sociology of

19 Karl Mannheim. *Essays on the Sociology of Knowledge.* New York : Oxford University Press, 1952. 327 pp.

20 Karl Mannheim. *Ideology And Utopia.* An Introduction to the Sociology of Knowledge. New York : Harcourt, Brace, 1959. 354 pp.

21 Karl Mannheim. *Essays On The Sociology Of Culture.* London : Routledge & Kegan, 1956. 253 pp.

knowledge. Modern scholarship has been fertile in applying the understanding of class and group ideologies to an analysis of historical events, in such areas as institutional economics, the social psychology of prejudice, attitude-formation and social stratification, industrial sociology and, of course, the analysis of social movements, whether the analysis be Marxist or non-Marxist in nature. Many other areas of modern scholarship bear witness to the insights that may be provided by an understanding of the motivations and dynamics of social aggregates.

In the same way an insight into the entire spectrum of forces which may move the individual, can deepen the understanding and analysis of the historian or of the non-historian who may be concerned with historical analysis. Some examples of historical analysis imbued with the viewpoint of philosophical anthropology, are to be found in Northrop's[22] "Philosophical Anthropology and Practical Politics," and infuse this author's analysis of such topics as Asian mentality and United States Foreign policy, modern ways in medieval societies, a discussion of the Sinhalese Experiment, man's relation to the earth in its bearing on his aesthetic, ethical, legal and political values, the present and likely future sucess of the Soviet Union, the remarkble short-run success of Mao's China, a discussion of the kind of modern eivilization that men may plump for, and the considerations that might be regarded as the normative ideals of a free people. Considerations from philosophical anthropology can clearly be ancillary to the historian's main functions, without in any sense becoming the content, itself of the historian's concerns. The more systematic concerns of philosophical anthropology proper have, of course, been explor-

22 F. S. C. Northrop. *Philosophical Anthropology & Practical Politics*. A Prelude To War Or To Just Law. New York : Macmillan. 1960. 384 pp.

ed by Scheler.[23]   What we are trying to emphasize here is that the *viewpoint* of Scheler, which calls for an integrated science of man, can enlarge the perspective of the professional historian in such a way that the fullest meaning of the behaviour of the historical actor will be caught up and, in consequence, the psychological dynamisms underlying momentous, individual historical decisions may be more easily recognized.

In adopting an existentialist perspective or a moral posture, the historian can hardly do justice to the flux of events without recognizing the roles played by "social atmospheres." I am referring to social contexts whose qualities are best described by such concepts as alienation, anomie, homogenization, bureaucratization, depersonalization and dehumanization. The historian is fully familiar with what is meant by alienation. The concept of alienation, however, seems to have been pre-empted by almost every other type of social scientist. It rarely appears as a working concept in the day to day concerns of the professional historian. Public opinion and public power are natural provinces of concern for the historian. Alienation is a morbid characteristic in both these contexts. It would be difficult, however, to find a historian who deals with the alienation to be found in the expression of public opinion and the exercise of public power, as we find alienation dealt with in these same two areas by Ortega y Gasset,[24] the Josephsons[25] or Marcel,[26] or even, for that matter, in the sense in which McLuhan[27] has unwittingly described the new forms of

23   Max Scheler. *Man's Place In Nature.* Boston : Beacon Press, 1961.   105 pp.

24   Jose Ortega y Gasset. *Man and People.* New York : W. W. Norton, 1957. 272 pp.

25   Eric and Mary Josephson. *Man Alone.* Alienation in Modern Society. New York : Dell, 1962.   592 pp.

26   Gabriel Marcel. *Men Against Humanity.* London : The Harvill Press, 1962. 205 pp.

27   Marshall McLuhan. *Understanding Media : The Extensions of Man.* New York : McGraw-Hill, 1964.   364 pp.

alienation that man's technological artifacts have ushered into being. So much, however, that represents historical tragedy has been in part the product of alienation that it seems almost absurd not to see many significant historical events against the background of the social atmosphere of alienation in which they took place. Alienation may exist in several forms : alienation from self, from the opposite sex, from one's fellow-man, from society, from work, from Nature and from the religious impulse. Surely historical perspective is enlarged when historical events are viewed against social atmospheres which, past or present, reflect one or another of these several forms of alienation.

When a society is left without norms for appropriate behaviour in a variety of important, social contexts, when ascribed roles seem to have become meaningless, when traditional standards appear to be irrelevant to current issues and crises and when there are no criteria by which groups, cultures and nations may guide their actions and refine the bases for social decision-making, then we have the social atmosphere which the sociologist refers to as *anomie*. From the historian's stand-point anomie is a *generalized, social rootlessness* and if such rootlessness eventuates in tragic and frustrating consequences for large, social groups, if it leads them into monumental errors and unnecessary conflict, then certainly the historian must take this into account. Where psychic and social disorgainzation are widespread they are as much the causes of historical change as, let us say, valid instances of economic determinism, the impacts of science and technology on institutional and economic life, or limited resources to and the struggle between nations for these.

The historian or the *non-historian* concerned with coming events, who shows a preference for existentialist interpretation, must not only be prepared to explain much of social change in terms of anomie but, even more, he should be prepared to forecast tentatively the direction and drift of events when an anomic social atmosphere prevails. This, in a sense, is what has been done to some extent in the work of Ellul [28],[29] and Seidenberg.[30],[31] It is not that these authors have directly addressed themselves to the analysis of the social atmosphere of anomie in our time. Rather they have chosen to deal with conditions which either currently generate anomie, as Ellul does, or with future conditions that may emerge, which are generated by current forms of anomie. What I am stressing here is that the professional historian can illuminate the social atmosphere of his own time by incorporating into his labours an interpretive point of view, changed with an existentialist awarenesss, that illuminates the social forces now at play by noting the extent to which they reflect anomie in his own time.

In the interpretation of the nature of cultures—what Cattell[32] has called "syntalities" by analogy with personalities—the existentialist outlook is almost imperative for the historian. The task of cultural interpretation, however, has become by default the province of the anthropologist and distinguished samples of work in this connection are some of the studies

28 Jacques Ellul. *The Technological Society*. New York : Alfred A. Knopf, 1964. 449 pp.

29 Jacques Ellul. *Propaganda*. The Formation of Men's Attitudes. New York : Alfred A. Knopf, 1965. 320 pp.

30 Roderick Seidenberg. *Post-Historic Man*. An Inquiry. Boston : Beacon Press, 1957. 246 pp.

31 Roderick Seidenberg. *Anatomy Of The Future*. Chapel Hill : The University of North Carolina Press, 1961. 173 pp.

32 Raymond B. Cattell. *Personality*. A Systematic Theoretical and Factual Study. New York : McGraw-Hill, 1950. 689 pp. See particularly chapter 14 "Personality And The Cultural Matrix : III. Group Dynamics And Personality," 386-417.

done by Benedict[33] and Mead.[34] Some social philosophers have also been busy in this connection, like Northrop.[35] A few writers, notably philosophers of history, have also cultivated the area of cultural interpretation rather extensively, notably Spengler[36] and Toynbee,[37] and the task of interpretating trends and ideas that move in the direction of *emerging world cultures*, has been courageously assumed by the historian, Wagar,[38] and to some extent, by specialists in American Civilization, like Lerner.[39]

What is the value of cultural interpretation to the historian, particularly when the "soul" of a culture can be examined with an existentialist bias ? The answer lies in this. To the extent that the notion is valid, that a culture or a civilization has a personality, a sort of statistically modal value-pattern, to that extent it has spiritual, that is, value-seeking boundaries. There are actions we can expect from it in a variety of situations, *actions that may be irrelevant* to a novel set of problems the culture in question faces, but actions which spring from the traditions (the achieved personality, so to speak) of that culture. And to the extent that Festinger's[40] concepts of *value-assonance* and *value-dissonance* are valid, there

---

33 Ruth Benedict. *Patterns Of Culture*. New York : Mentor Books, 1953. 272 pp.

34 Margaret Mead *Sex And Temperament In Three Primitive Societies*. New York : Mentor Books, 1960. 218 pp.

35 F. C. S. Northrop. *The Meeting Of East And West*. New York : Macmillan, 1958. 531 pp.

36 Oswald Spengler. *The Decline Of The West*. New York : Alfred E. Knopf, 1945. New revised edition. 2 vols.

37 Arnold Toynbee. *A Study Of History*. London : Oxford University Press. 12 vols. 1935-1961.

38 W. Warren Wagar. *Op. cit.*

39 Max Lerner. *America As A Civilization*. Life And Thought In The United States Today. New York : Simon and Schuster, 1957. 1036 pp.

40 Leon Festinger. *A Theory Of Cognitive Dissonance*. Evanston, Illinois : Row, Peterson, 1957. 291 pp.

are values which are incompatible with the syntality of a civilization. Because this is so, there are actions which would clearly be against the grain of a culture, even when such actions may be necessary for its survival. Toynbee has, of course, recognized and this recognition has prompted him to stress the fact that many cultures have perished because of inability to adapt to novel circumtances in their "times of trouble." The type of interpretation we get from Toynbee, it seems to me, has unparalleled value for the professional historian. Toynbee has often viewed cultural inelasticity from the viewpoint of Christianity. What I am suggesting is that if the historian combines a sense of cultural pattern and cultural rigidity with some of the basic modes of analysis in existentialism, he can provide a canvas possessing even greater insights than Toynbee's composition of culture-consciousness and the Christian outlook.

Existentialism also lends itself very well to the presentation of an interpretative pluralism in the writing of history. The ability to look at the same events from a variety of perspectives can be an advantage in historical explanation, although, naturally, this would be regarded as a decided disadvantage by the historiographer seeking "maximum objectivity." Generally a variety of perspectives almost invariably involves a variety of values on the part of the interpreters involved, and this will be true whether the values are made explicit or are only implicit. A perfect example of the value of multiple perspectives on the interpretation of the impact which current science and technology are having on our lives, would be to compare the views of McLuhan,[41] Seidenberg[42] and Mumford.[43]

---

41 Marshall McLuhan. *Op. cit.*

42 Roderick Seidenberg. *Op. cit.*

43 Lewis Mumford. *Technics and Civilization.* New York and Burlingame : Harcourt, Brace & World, 1963. 495 pp.

The ability certainly to appreciate this multiplicity of viewpoints is enhanced by a sensitivity to the manner in which science and technology produce changes in the *inner life* of individuals and cultures. This sensitivity may be present in non-existentialists as well as those who identify themselves with some form or other of existentialism. The historian who is open to an appreciation of these varied forms of sensitivity and who sees value in the deliberate employment of existentialist modes of awareness in trying to analyze historical change, possesses a certain advantage. He can empathetically and appreciatively put himself in the position demanded by each of the modes of interpretation that he has given his attention and he can look at the same historical events from the vantage point of these different modes, without in any way sacrificing accuracy. The values for his reader, of the presentation of such multiple modes of viewing the same historical events, is, I think, immeasureable.

The existentialist is overwhelmingly preoccupied with questions of value—personal and social—and were the historian to reflect an existentialist outlook, he could not possibly avoid describing and critically examining segments of the prevailing value-patterns of his own community when the life of that community is the focus of his attention. Although in no sense an existentialist in his outlook, the historian, Baritz,[44] has executed an example of the type of study we have in mind here. Baritz has chosen to deal with the history of the abuses that have emerged in this country in management's decision to apply the findings and techniques of the social sciences to industry and business. But Baritz has done this as an *intellectual* and not as an existentialist. Still, it must be recognized that the *moral concerns* of existentialists do tend to be reflected by many

---

44 Loren Baritz. *Op. cit.*

100

intellectuals, perhaps by most of them, including even those intellectuals who may be strongly critical of one or another of the convictions and outlooks found in the many forms of contemporary existentialism. The intellectual, as historian or social critic, must be given separate attention precisely because his moral criticisms and postures often parallel those of committed existentialists. As an intellectual imbued with the concerns for the moral importance of social reconstruction and greatly influenced by the desire to help usher into being a more perfect and more just social order, Baritz has stated what he believes to be the true moral and social functions of an intellectual and he has stated these in a way in which the historian with an existentialist viewpoint might easily accept them. Hofstadter[45] has pithily summed up the intellectual's credo, as Baritz sees it and I can do no better than to quote at this point this summation from Hofstadter.

...a young historian Loren Baritz, looking at the social disciplines from a similar point of view, expounded the belief that "any intellectual who accepts and approves of his society prostitutes his skills and is a traitor to his heritage." He asked whether, "by definition, a man of ideas must maintain the posture of the critic, and whether the intellectual who sincerely believes in and approves of the larger movements of his society can reconcile the demands of his mind and those of his society." He called for a principled withdrawal of intellectuals from social institutions, from relevance, responsibility, and power : "Let the intellectual be absorbed into society and he runs the grave risk of permitting himself to be digested by it.... When he touches power, it will touch him." The right response is a willed estrangement from social responsibility : "When the intellectal becomes socially, rather than intellectually, responsible his mind must lose at least part of the freedom and resiliency which is part of his most fundamental equipment." If the intellectual withdraws to the ivory tower, it is because of "this need for social irresponsibility, for irrelevancy, for the freedom which comes from isolation and alienation" (397-98).

---

45 Richard Hofstadter. *Op. cit.*

While we are on the subject of intellectuals with an existentialist viewpoint—regardless of whether they apply the rubric of "existentialist" to themselves—let us note that the manner in which an existentialist posture tends to be exhibited by the modern critical intellectual, may be easily seen in the early work of Benda[46] who addressed himself to pre-World War II intellectuals and who pleaded with them to perform their true functions by adopting the postures advocated in the selection from Hofstadter, quoted above. One sees again this posture as it has been exercised by the busy intellectual with an existentialist passion for decency and justice in the biography of the famous German, anti-Nazi intellectual, Schoenberner.[47] By contrast with Baritz's conviction that the intellectual should abstain from being absorbed in partisan, political action, we must note that there have been some intellectuals who have felt that total immersion in political action and power is the *central, moral duty* of the committed intellectual.

The lives and views of three such intellectuals, Leon Blum, Walther Rathenau and F. T. Marinetti, have been described by Joll.[48] The concern that must be emphasized here, of course, is the recognition that there is a deep relationship between the religious impulse and the movement of social change and that the historian's profeessional abilities are amplified when he is highly sensitized to this fact. This will be true whether or not he calls himself an existentialist. Two noted examples of the recognition of this relationship and an extended use of it prof-

46 Julien Benda. *The Betrayal Of The Intellectuals.* Boston : The Beacon Press, 1955. 188 pp.

47 Franz Schoenberner. *Confession Of A European Intellectual.* New York : Collier Books, 1965. 338 pp.

48 James Joll. *Three Intellectuals In Politics.* New York : Harper & Row, 1965. 203 pp.

essionally are to be found, for instance, in the work of the historian, Dawson.[49],[50]

Because of the intimate and often parallel relationship between the intellectual as a social critic and the existentialist as a social critic, the historian who wishes to deploy sympathetically the social and moral criticisms which are so frequently among the central themes of existentialism, should certainly familiarize himself with the role, status and value-schemas of intellectuals. A knowledge of intellectual history is, of course, part of the standard equipment of the professional historian, but intellectual history is essentially a preoccupation with the nature and effect of ideas on society, as these ideas are directly stated and elaborated upon, or intellectual history may be executed in the form of an analysis of the *Zeitgeist* as that *Zeitgeist* is expressed in the realm of ideas and through literature. Intellectual history may, of course, be a mixture of both these modes of analysis. A well-known and highly scholarly example of the first category is the work of Randall.[51] A brief and *popular* treatment of the historical significance of ideas is found in the work of Robinson.[52] A preoccupation with the role of ideas in U. S. history is illustrated in a well-known sourcebook edited by Commager[53]—a sourcebook whose material makes a *demand* upon the reader that is intermediate be-

---

49 Christopher Dawson. *The Dynamics Of World History.* New York : Mentor Books, 1962. 477 pp.

50 Christopher Dawson. *Progress And Religion.* New York : Doubleday, 1960. 200 pp.

51 John Herman Randall, Jr. *The Making Of The Modern Mind.* Boston : Houghton Mifflin, 1940. 696 pp.

52 James Harvey Robinson. *The Mind In The Making.* London : C. A. Watts & Co. Ltd., 1949. 148 pp.

53 Henry Steele Commager (Editor). *Living Ideas In America.* New York : Harper, 1951. 766 pp.

6

tween the effort required by Randall and that required by Robinson. Two well-known scholarly examples of a treatment of the history of ideas, chiefly in terms of their expression in literature, are found in the scholarly contributions of Highet[54] and Huizinga.[55]

I am, however, not talking about the historian's preoccupation with ideas in any form. I am instead talking about the *progenitors* of ideas, the intellectuals, themselves, the figures whose moral criticisms of the human condition are either similar to or identical with those made in the mainstream of existentialist writings, whether these latter be literary or otherwise. The type of existentialist criticism to which I am referring here is the type that has been undertaken by Barrett[56] and which has been expressed, *in part*, by Wild.[57] Intellectuals with moral conmitments tend to make criticisms that are somewhat parallel in spirit to those of Barrett and Wild. There has been a recent revival of concern with the intellectual and with his role, status and moral obligations to society. Benda'[58] Coser,[59] Molnar,[60] Schoenberner,[61] Aron,[62] Lasch[63] and Feuer[64] are

54 Gilbert Highet. *The Classical Tradition*. Greek And Roman Influences On Western Literature. New York : Oxford University Press. 1957. 763 pp.

55 J. Huizinga. *The Waning of the Middle Ages*. New York : Doubleday, 1954. 362 pp.

56 William Barrett. *Irrational Man*. A Study in Existential Philosophy. New York : Doubleday, 1958. 278 pp.

57 John Wild. *Op. cit.*

58 Julien Benda. *Op. cit.*

59 Lewis Coser. *Men Of Ideas*. A Sociologist's View. New York : The Free Press, 1965. 374 pp.

60 Thomas Molnar. *The Decline of the Intellectual*. Cleveland and New York : World Publishing Co., Meridian Books, 1961. 369 pp.

61 Franz Schoenberner. *Op. cit.*

62 Raymond Aron. *The Opium of the Intellectuals*. New York : Norton, 1962. 324 pp.

63 Christopher Lasch. *The New Radicalism in America (1889-1963)*. The Intellectual as a Social Type. New York : Alfred A. Knopf, 1965. 349 pp.

64 Lewis S. Feuer. *The Scientific Intellectual*. The Psychological & Sociological Origins of Modern Science. New York : Basic Books, 1963. 441 pp.

among some of the contemporary figures who have displayed the concern with intellectuals of which I now speak. In the work of the men just mentioned we are given a clear picture of the moral commitment of the intellectual and of the manner in which that commitment emerges as a criticism of society. It is to that commitment and to the appreciation of the intellectual's concern for a more just social order that, I think, the historian must lend a sympathetic ear. If in the evaluation of contemporary, historical trends the historian can reflect that same sense of moral commitment and employ the social ideals of the intellectuals as benchmarks against which to evaluate current and emerging trends, the lessons of history will thereby be rendered more significant. Derivatively too, the existentialist posture to a large extent will come to life and will come to life to the degree that the social and moral criticism of the intellectuals parallels the affective concerns of existentialists.

As a moral critic of society and, in general, of the human condition, and as a proxy for the conceptual schemas of existentialism, the historian should also sharpen his focus of evaluation by a familiarity with social criticism that is value-oriented and humanistically laden, where such criticism has been exercised by professionals in other fields. The type of critical perspective to which I am alluding here is exemplified in the work of such sociologists as Mills,[65,66] Riesman [67,68,69]

65 · C. Wright Mills. *The Power Elite*. New York : Oxford University Press, 1956. 423 pp.

66 C. Wright Mills. *The Causes Of World War Three*. New York : Simon and Schuster, 1938. 172 pp.

67 David Riesman et al. *The Lonely Crowd*. A Study of the Changing American Character. New York : Doubleday, 1953. 359 pp.

68 David Riesman. *Individnalism Reconsidered*. Glencoe, Illinois. The Free Press, 1954. 529 pp.

69 David Riesman. *Abundance For What ?* New York : Doubleday, 1964. 610 pp.

and Sorokin,[70] in the work of such an existentially oriented humanist as Arendt [71] or in the work of a classic type of humanist like Ortega y Gasset,[72] and in the work of an economist such as Boulding.[73] These figures *are illustrative* only. Literally thousands of examples could be drawn from other fields. And inasmuch as contemporary history and the emerging future will be predominantly affected by the innovations in science and technology in the West, the historian with an existentialist "bias"— if that is the right word — must become aware of the way in which technology produces its own imperatives, as elaborated upon by Ellul.[74] He must therefore be prepared to describe the plight of the individual against the backdrop of the imperatives of technology.

Under the hardening social influence of science and technology the insights of existentialism are more needed than ever before, if man's artifacts are to serve rather than to crush him. The historian is advantageously equipped to unfold the drama of social change from an existentialist viewpoint and thereby evaluate its compulsions and directions. When such evaluation is self-consciously pursued in a professional sense and yet executed without doing violence to the facts of history, of social movements and of social processes, the importation of an existentialist vantage point into historiography will be all to the good. Full-blooded efforts along such lines can, perhaps, best be done through the collaboration of sophisticated

70 Pitirim A. Sorokin. *The Crisis Of Our Age*. The Social And Cultural Outlook. New York : E. P. Dutton, 1941. 338 pp.

71 Hannah Arendt. *The Human Condition*. A Study Of The Central Dilemmas Facing Modern Man. New York : Doubleday, 1959. 385 pp.

72 Jose Ortega y Gasset. *The Revolt Of The Masses*. New York : Norton, 1957. 190 pp.

73 Kenneth Boulding. *The Meaning of the 20th Century*. The Great Transition. New York : Harper & Row, 1964. 199 pp.

74 Jacques Ellul. *Op. cit.*

existentialists and professional historians. I suspect, however, that the treatment of historical themes can be more successfully vitalized when the large-scale abstractions of the historian and his traditional penchant for the depersonalized, "objective" approach are balanced against the insights and concerns of an existentialist perspective. The value of the blend we are emphasizing here, however, can be judged only in terms of the professional work that will be done under its aegis in the years that life ahead.

PART IV: EFFECTS OF THE FRAMEWORK OF VALUES UPON OUTLOOK AND BEHAVIOR

THE EDUCATION OF CONSCIOUSNESS

In a very fundamental sense education consists of all our efforts to enlarge the horizons of man's consciousness. When educational theory is propounded in these terms, the writer almost invariably thinks solely of increasing intellectual perceptiveness. This stress is due to several fairly independent factors which converge to over-determine it. One contributory factor is the early separation in the history of natural philosophy, of questions of fact from questions of value. This separation has had a signal triumph in the physical sciences and so successful has been the strictly cognitive approach to an effort to understand both ourselves and the world, that it has led to extreme forms of scientism in modern behavioral and social science theory. Only recently has a concerted effort arisen to ascertain more cautiously whether, in fact, cryptic value stances lie hidden in all those areas of research which are preoccupied with animate and social forms. In fact some have begun to challenge the very assumption that much is to be gained *always* by separating questions of fact from questions of value. A conviction has arisen in some quarters that there may be areas of inquiry where in fact this cannot be done and other areas of inquiry where perhaps it should not be done. Doubts are systematically developed in the writings of such men as Myrdal (3) and Polanyi (4) and in approaches of a phenomenological and existential nature such as we see in philosophy, existential psychiatry and cognitive psychology.

Another factor contributing to the identification of the enlargement of consciousness with sheer intellectual power, comes from the analytical successes of the philosophy of science. There is so much of what Jerome Bruner (2) calls "effective surprise" that comes from successful model-building, mathematical analysis, linguistic reconstruction and successful hypothesis-formation, that the young lover of learning finds his head is easily turned. He fastens upon these devices because they structure situations highly for him. Life, itself, leaves so many problems and situations so highly *unstructured*, that it is a relief to turn to those small and comfortable research contexts which promise to eliminate all ambiguity for us. As a result the range of attention shrinks to the strictly cognitive aspects of consciousness and the holistic tendencies of man, which the Greeks clung to so stubbornly and tenaciously, are lost sight of completely.

A third factor tending to make us feel that when we speak of

THE JOURNAL OF EDUCATIONAL SOCIOLOGY, Dec. 1962, vol. 36, 185-189.

enhancing consciousness, we have reference only to logico-empirical forms of inquiry, is the fact that, of all forms of consciousness, this is the most publicly communicable of all. It is only in the exercise of logico-empirical forms of inquiry that communication is most *completely* public or as the philosophers of science put it, definitely inter-subjective. This fosters the illusion that what makes for such a high degree of shared experience is tantamount to the only kind of experience with which consciousness can traffic. Since shared consciousness of this type aids and abets the most successful manipulation of our human environments and makes possible the great technology which has transformed human history, we find it easy to convince ourselves that only this type of shared communion is real. As Bergmann (1) has so interestingly pointed out in analyzing the psychological biases underlying a radical empiricism, these constitute a form of massive repression by which we succeed in making ourselves forget that the rational is often only a highly refined form of the intuitive.

I do not wish to leave the reader with the impression that these are the only or even major historical factors which have led to the conviction that rational cognition is all there is to consciousness. There are unquestionably other determining factors. What I do wish to do, however, is to suggest that there is a wider taxonomy of consciousness for educational effort than these traditional assumptions would lead us to believe. It is my own conviction that there are at least five types of consciousness which educational effort can seek to foster. These are dialectical consciousness, empathic consciousness, value consciousness, methodological consciousness and holistic or integrative consciousness. I should like to characterize these as briefly as possible below.

Dialectic consciousness makes us fit for articulate and profound communication. It is characterized by being a balanced blend of logic, semantics and a sense of the value system and metaphysics which underly the manner in which we actually propose to pursue the good life, to contemplate it or to criticise it. It enables us to examine all aspects of an issue or problem and yet never lose sight of the core meanings predicated by that problem and which nevertheless influence its peripheral aspects.

Empathic consciousness is concerned with developing techniques for the thorough intellectual understanding of the other person's predicament, for developing in ourselves the feelings with which that predicament becomes charged and a show of compassion for the individual in that predicament, which the occasion requires. Add to this the recognition that the sufferer is ourself in another corporeal frame and add the earnest wish to eliminate that suffering by one means or another, and we come closer to what is involved in empathy. Add further that in a psychological sense we feel we are our brother's keeper and that a workable morality of sentiment and feeling demands that we help the other fellow to grow and realize himself, both when he is aware of his conflicts and frustrations and when he is not, and the cup of empathy is nearly full. Ideally there should be no limit to the mutual aid which empathic consciousness involves. We may fall short of how much empathy we can give but we must do no bookkeeping in advance as to the amount of empathic credit we are prepared to extend. We give what our limitations, circumstances and insight allow us to give, no less and no more.

Value consciousness arises when we make a conscious effort, both intellectually and emotionally, to translate the pattern of values to which we subscribe, into action, either in relation to our own personal growth, in relation to the growth and needs of our fellowmen, in relation to our human ecology, that is, Nature, or in relation to the unresolved mysteries of life and matter which is sometimes called the sense of the mystery of Being. We must commit ourselves to actions which fulfill or implement the values we profess, and if we clearly understand the implication of our values we may understand what these implications demand in action for a variety of contexts. It is this type of commitment which philosophical existentialists stress and which they describe as a resolve to "engage ourselves." We must seriously avoid a gap between the values we hold and the behavior which so often works against them. It is this difference between conceived and operative values which marks the greater insanity of our time, in contrast with human behavior in the past. This gap is widening rather than narrowing with middlebrow culture whose most characteristic feature is to cultivate as a virtue the socially approved schizophrenia of our time. This it succeeds in doing very largely through the widespread, smug appreciation of role-playing. The psychologist, Festinger, calls the awareness of the fitness of our actions and our values, cognitive assonance. When we develop cognitive assonance we are developing one sense of value consciousness. When we are almost completely unaware what we mean by our values, even verbally, and when we are almost completely unaware that our actions are out of joint with our expressed values, even where we are clear as to what these mean, we suffer from cognitive dissonance which is the absence of value consciousness entirely.

One of the essentials for escaping superficiality of understanding, is to cultivate a capacity to think clearly and to think scientifically. The first is generally a product of the development of logical and semantic penetration into the issues which move us. The second is an awareness of the manner in which research must be undertaken or designed in order to arrive at natural or social truth. If we add to these an awareness of the metaphysical and value presuppositions which underly even our scientific ventures and an awareness of the relationships between our theoretical constructions and the world as given, we have what I am calling *methodological* consciousness. Taking all these matters in the aggregate, we can speak of them as the "philosophy of science." A good familiarity with the philosophy of science and a readiness to approach problems of human communication in its terms, together with the realization that systematic inquiry into anything demands a deep and firm understanding of scientific method, will save us from much error and frustration and certainly from middlebrow confusion. Deliberate efforts to function in these terms represents what is meant by methodological consciousness.

Finally no real cultivation of intellect and spirit and no intelligent employment of action is possible without integrative or holistic consciousness. This refers to the studied effort on our part to avoid compartmentalization of different theories concerning the same phenomenon or the fragmentation of knowledge into disparate data whose relationships do not arouse our interest. When we make an effort to coordinate *different theories* dealing with the same or different aspects of a common problem or phenomenon, this is one type of integrative consciousness, particularly when the coordination achieves a new theoretical unity. When we coordinate *different data* which are related to each other, so as to see the relevance of these data to a common phenomenon or problem, we have a second type of integrative consciousness. The first we call coordinative integration and the second existential integration. The two types together make up integrative consciousness. When integrative consciousness is deliberately cultivated in our contacts both with human knowledge and theory and in our experience with different aspects of nature and self, we have laid another brick in the temple of human development and we have added another weapon to the armory with which we can avoid educated obtuseness.

If each of us takes seriously an education devoted to the development of these five types of consciousness, we can make sense of our common concern with the good life. If not, we shall continue to develop an increasing state of confusion and a deepening sense of the disjointedness of all our experience. For such a situation the proper epitaph would be "the left hand knoweth not what the right hand doeth." No education which seeks to understand the human spirit whole can afford to approve of such a denouement.

REFERENCES

1. Bergmann, G. Philosophy of Science. Madison: Univ. Wisconsin Press, 1957. Pp. 181.
2. Bruner, J. S. On Knowing. Essays for the Left Hand. Cambridge: The Belknap Press of Harvard U. Press, 1962. Pp. 165.
3. Myrdal, G. Value in Social Theory. A Selection of Essays on Methodology (edited by Paul Streeten). New York: Harper, 1958. Pp. 269.
4. Polanyi, M. Personal Knowledge. Towards a Post-Critical Philosophy, Chicago: The U. Chicago Press, 1958. Pp. 428.

CAN WE EDUCATE FOR A SENSE OF VALUE?

Over the course of the years the average college educator must often wonder why the values to which his students have given lip-service in the classroom seem so often not to have been adhered to in their later behavior as citizens. This observation has surely had its dramatic impact on many of us where we have had an opportunity to follow the later careers of some of our students. Perhaps even more impressive is the sense of bewilderment and frustration which overcomes each of us when we observe the gap and, often, also the conflict between the values expressed by a colleague and his behavior as one of a company of scholars. We are all familiar with the educator who is full of mouth-filling phrases about democracy but who unhesitatingly supports authoritarian, administrative procedures within his own academic institution and who will happily work night and day to maintain a going oligocracy. We are all familiar with the educator who stands over a public rostrum and delivers himself of twaddle concerning the need for a well-rounded, liberal education and then, given the power to reward and punish, fiercely devotes his energies to encouraging the narrowest of specialization among his associates, rationalizing his behavior in terms of "the need to develop professional competence." Each of us has met sometime in his life the educator whose textbook makes a plea for eclecticism in theory or social point of view but whose choice of friends among associates is overdetermined by the question of whether or not they share his professional biases. Likewise it is not rare to meet the self-styled classroom and campus "liberal" whose views on social, political, and economic matters are invariably conservative with a vengeance and whose inconsistencies are not a matter of semantics. Many more such inconsistencies between values and behavior than the foregoing might be cited; but to do so would be superfluous here, for the reader

JOURNAL OF HUMANISTIC PSYCHOLOGY, Spring 1961, vol. 1, 35-47.

can draw upon memory and experience to supply an ample set of additions for himself.

Our educators were also once students. Like so many of our students who have taken up non-educational careers, our educators also exhibit a tremendous difference between their expressed values and their actual behavior. What are some of the omissions and failures in the practices of modern higher education which may tend to produce such socially and professionally approved schizophrenic behavior? There are several factors which must be held to account, besides going practices of higher education, and undoubtedly some of these have gotten in their licks before our students ever get to us. In what way, however, can higher education be held to be an accessory to the fact? The chief cause, I believe, which contributes to the division we manifest between expressed values and behavior, is psychological neglect. We have failed to take stock of those psychological processes which are intimately bound up with the mental activity of value-discrimination and choice. We have also failed to give sufficient serious concern to those psychological roots of personal and social behavior which would enable us to reflect or contravene our declared values. I should like then to turn to a discussion of these major psychological factors for the light which such a discussion might shed on our current inabilities to educate for values and the opportunities we miss to reinforce a sense of value where the individual has a general but vague sense of what constraints his value-system imposes on his prospective behavior.

In the development of a sense of value, the first difficulty which the average human being faces is, I should say, semantic. For many it is not clear what the meaning of a value-statement or a value-outlook may be. The referent of a value-assertion is clearly one or more samples of our prospective behavior over the course of time. However, when human beings declare their values, the statements asserted tend to be elliptically formulated; that is to say, the declaration of a value tends to be context-free. This ellipsis, along with other possibilities which may invest an asserted value with ambiguity, makes the task of determining the implied behavior very confusing. Consider the ambiguities which are inherent in so familiar a statement (asserted value) as the following. "The democratic way of life is most conducive to individual and social development." This statement is not surrounded with qualifications. The young seeker, whether college student or not, who has not achieved a level of maturity which will furnish a critical outlook, does not notice several aspects of linguistic obscurity which impoverish the meaning of the statement in question. (1) There is no specification of the circumstances or of other entailed values, under which the statement might be either true or false. (2) The statement is treated as an absolute, that is <u>true</u> <u>for</u> <u>all</u> <u>time</u>, in the form given. (3) The main term, "democracy" is almost completely subjective, evoking, to use a phrase borrowed from the general semanticists, different <u>klang</u> associations for each person who hears it. (4) The statement does not specify which forms of individual and social development may be desirable and which undesirable. (5) As an appeal to experience the statement represents a bias masquerading as an empirical falsehood. Neither history nor experiment can bear testimony to its truth; that is to say, some historically known communities which men have called "democratic," such as the colonial, Puritan, New England community, have stifled individual and social development, if the objective judgments of historian and psychologist are to be taken seriously. On the other hand, oligocracies and hereditary principalities, such as those of the Venetian city states, have at times been associated with a tremendous flourishing of individual and social growth.

There are still other shortcomings attending the determination of the meaning of our statement concerning democracy, which we shall gloss over as minor in the context of the present discussion. The important point to be made in connection with the meaning of assertions of value is that many of them are equivocal and often much more so than the particular example we have used above. This being so, those of us who try to live by them uncritically may easily fall into the trap of exhibiting behavior which does not appear to exemplify the value in question in the eyes of an observer who may have given specific content to an assertion of value. This he may have done by deliberately removing as much equivocality from the assertion, as possible, and structuring its meaning for a variety of contexts. If others have not done likewise, obviously they run the risk of exhibiting behavior which, in the eyes of a critical observer, is clearly inconsistent with our expressed values.

There are, of course, few deliberate attempts made in higher education today to invest the undergraduate with skills at semantic analysis and to encourage their application to the most cherished values we live by. By this I mean that the propositions of value which are met with everywhere in political science, sociology, applied and industrial psychology, history, philosophy and the humanities, are not subjected in the classroom to this type of analysis. Systems of value borrowed in whole or in part from the classroom atmosphere in which these subjects are taught are pocketed with all their ambiguity and all their uncertainty of referred-to-behavior, when they are parroted elliptically. Our educational failure in this respect results from several causes: an emphasis on the acquisition of information, a failure to distinguish assertions of value from assertions of fact, the desire to treat our specialties as source material for social nostrums, our own intellectual laziness and naivete, an abdication of duty because of lack of dedication to all aspects of our field and sometimes an ignorance of the power of Socratic Method. Sometimes we fail to stress the importance of an analysis of assertions of value because of a strong sense of the cultural resistance against developing an appreciation of the value of analysis in examining the major convictions we live by. We despair because of the anti-intellectual attitudes of so many of our students and the widespread depreciation in which learning and the profound examination of issues are held. Then again the failure may be a result of timidity or perhaps of prudence. There is always the risk that community sentiment may be violated by the analysis of widely held values and that if such analysis is noted without any understanding of the intention behind it, it is likely to be treated as subversive. Prudence often dictates that we abdicate professional ideals on the ground that unemployed educators are non-educators, while employed educators may be, at least, partial educators. Cultural and religious pressures may make educational expediency and opportunism the order of the day.

The most frequent failure to develop a functional sense of value, however, arises not from linguistic and semantic difficulties but, rather, from what the Gestalt psychologist would call cognitive deficiency. Cognitive deficiency will occur when a subject interprets a value-assertion for one or two contexts, say politics and family life, yielding clear-cut attitudes with respect to prospective behavior for these two realms. However, the subject does not interpret the value-assertion in question for other contexts. From the standpoint of the subject the meaning and intention of the asserted value are clear.

The subject can represent to himself mentally the implications in behavior in quite great detail for a large variety of circumstances in one or two categorized contexts, say economics, politics, or education; but he has never taken the trouble to spell these out mentally for a variety of circumstances in other contexts. Furthermore, he has developed the appropriate dispositions which support the value in context A, and is completely lacking in the proper dispositions to reinforce the same value in context B. When a subject's interpretations of a value-assertion are made for the major contexts in which human beings relate to one another, we can speak of an approximation to the explicit possession of a complete, cognitive, value-pattern. When the individual fails to interpret a statement of value for one or more of these major contexts, we speak of the cognitive isolation of these contexts. Cognitive isolation is certainly one of the more conspicuous situations which give rise to subsequent behavior incongruous with our major assertions of value. Many factors in our lives produce cognitive isolation, but among the leading determinants are intellectual laziness, lack of interest in a given context, and relative indifference to contexts of experience remote in either space or time, or both. Most educators, unfortunately, do not have the right or the time to create cognitive coherence for a value among a variety of circumstances which may arise in one given context; and even less do they have the privilege of developing homogeneity of value for a cognitive pattern which would interweave a variety of the major social contexts of our lives. These tasks are peculiarly the province of the individual in the face of his accumulating experience. Exceptions concerning the function of the professional educator must be made for the professor of philosophy, education, or religion, but the overwhelming majority of our students do not elect studies in these areas. The development of cognitive isolation, then, is not at present so much a failure of higher education as it is a failure in individual, personal development.

There are two major approaches which may be recommended to enhance the role of higher education in this connection. A conservative approach would be to make courses in philosophy, social philosophy, ethics and kindred subjects, mandatory for all. This, of course, would at best make the development of value-consciousness a happy accident, and a happy accident for probably a very small minority. A more radical approach would be to develop programs of integrated education which are not restricted only to the synthesis of information and skills in relation to understanding and problem-solving, but which also take the development of consciousness of value in all its ramifications as a major objective.

Let us now suppose that an individual is relatively free from semantic confusion and cognitive isolation with respect to his values. Are there still other considerations which may make a mockery of one's value-system? Unfortunately there are. Writers in the field of value-theory distinguish between an individual's conceived and operative values; that is, between the clarity with which he intellectually represents the meaning of a value and the degree to which his behavior in a variety of contexts is in conformity with that value. This conformity is not to be confused with cognitive coherence. This last has to do with the extent to which a value is spelled out mentally, in terms of prospective behavior in a variety of contexts in which behavior can be exhibited which could exemplify in action the meaning of an asserted value. It is concerned with how completely the individual has represented the possible meanings of the value for the major modes of human existence. Suppose, however, an individual has represented to himself the meaning of a value for political behavior. It does not follow, of course, that his subsequent political behavior will jibe with this representation; for such matters as social habit, thoughtlessness, prejudice, social pressure, conflicts of loyalty, and unfamiliarity with specific, novel situations which may arise for the individual, all may contribute to the social judgment that an individual's actions conflict with his expressed value. There may be no semantic or cognitive error involved in the representation of the value for a political context, although clearly there can be inconsistency between each of several acts in a major category of human behavior and the representation of the asserted value for this category. Frequently one's political values stem from a more general and overarching value or set of values; and when the cognitive representation in this major area (politics in the present example) is, itself, as equivocal and elliptical as the overarching value from which it stems, the possibility for behavioral inconsistency is increased. This will be particularly true when that behavior is judged by others who have reduced or eliminated the equivocality of the general value for themselves and for the derivative major context. Inconsistency between one's behavior and one's asserted value, then, can occur in one or both of the foregoing senses.

The psychologist, Festinger, has dealt with what he calls cognitive dissonance, namely, meanings among represented values which do not cohere with one another. This is an element of value confusion of prime importance in itself and which we are glossing over in the present discussion because it deserves separate treatment. Festinger has devoted himself to research on this type of value confusion in his volume, A Theory of Cognitive Dissonance. Paraphrasing Festinger's terminology we wish to speak here of the inconsistency between the individual's cognition of a value and his behavior, as this behavior is judged by others, as value-dissonance. The agreement between the representation of the value and behavior we shall call value-assonance. Where value-assonance has been achieved, I believe the individual tends to be both conceptually integrated (which is the same as saying that he shows a great deal of cognitive assonance, the phrase used by Festinger) in respect to his conceived values, and behaviorally integrated in that he shows a pronounced tendency to act out or reflect these values properly. This double-barreled disposition not only serves his own growth and development, but also serves to promote altruistically the development of other personalities. Historical personalities with a high degree of value-assonance have been rare. St. Francis of Assisi, acting out the commandment to "love thy neighbor as thyself"; Voltaire, acting out the Enlightenment principle of tolerance by defending the Huguenots against persecution; in our own time, Prince Kropotkin making personal sacrifices to give substance to the concept of "mutual aid"; or Albert Schweitzer devoting almost all of his time to activities which are assonant to his concept of "reverence of life"—are all cases in point. Unfortunately, however, value-dissonance is the rule for most of us. Why should this be so?

One of the major factors producing value-dissonance, which every educator has had the opportunity to observe among both students and colleagues, occurs when the assertion of a value possesses only verbal content. In short, it results from the adoption of what Riesman calls "other-orientedness," which prompts us to indulge in parrot-like repetition of the value cliches of those groups with which we are psychologically affiliated, without even bothering to give our value-assertions, as such, intellectual content. These assertions, then, amount to a technique of reinforcing our sense of belonging and acceptance. An assertion of this sort is an acoustic badge and nothing more. A second consideration which promotes value-dissonance will arise when an individual is only intellectually committed to a value or a set of cohering values. This type of cause is rather widespread and, by virtue of the emphasis on role-playing so characteristic of status-conscious cultures, it constitutes the most widely approved form of social schizophrenia in our time. It is this socially approved schizophrenia which has been the despair of the existentialists and which has given rise to the insistence among them that "man must engage himself" with values and "commit" himself in action to their realization. As educators we fail to the extent that we do not check into the degree to which the student has made a value intellectually comprehensible to himself rather than remain content with verbally parroting it in order to provide self-reinforced evidence that he belongs. Where superficiality of conviction, of allegiance and of education are the rule—the great middlebrow vice of our time—strictly verbal expressions of value will be commonplace. This is inescapable, for they are of a piece with other types of behavior which enact role-playing conformity and which, more important still, prevent the appearance of socio-psychological anguish and tension, both of which are inevitable concomitants of genuine growth. Intellectually empty value-assertions then facilitate role-playing; and where the educator does not lead the student through Socratic questioning to make clear to himself at least the intellectual content of a value-assertion, he is derelict in his duty. As educators we probably also fail where, even though the student is clear as to the conceptual content of a value-expression, we make no effort to check on whether his values are expressed in his own personal way of life. Extended friendly inquiry of this sort might reveal those actions of the student which violate his declared values and those aspects of his personal life which call for activity in fulfillment of these values. If we fail as educators in these respects, our failure is possibly the price we pay for overemphasizing the acquisition of facts and the demand that the student regurgitate these, together with our explicit classroom biases. It is important that we check to see whether the values which inhere in the subject matter have, in fact, become part of the living warp and woof of the developing student.

There are, of course, other causes for value-dissonance. Outright dishonesty in the individual is one of these, and here little responsibility can be placed upon the shoulders of the educator. This dishonesty, when highly characteristic, may have been formed by the individual's family or peer group and is part of the investment in behavior with which the student arrives at the university's doors. As we have already remarked, psychological conflicts will also produce value-dissonance. These conflicts generally arise from cognitive dissonance of which the individual is quite aware, and the variety of ways in which the individual tries to reduce this dissonance or eliminate it from the center of attention is a central consideration in Festinger's A Theory of Cognitive Dissonance. We leave the solution of such conflicts, on the whole, to the psychiatrist, the clinical psychologist and, in an academic setup, to the institutional counselor. In recent years the counseling of students has been on the increase. When such counseling is of high professional caliber, this is all to the good. It reduces somewhat the tendency to value-dissonance. However, many counselors, in or out of universities, are, themselves, the product of cognitive dissonance. Such counselors then become sources of infection themselves, aggravating the value-pathology of our time. It is not the university's function to pass judgment upon the spiritual wholeness (value-assonance), individuality (as contrasted with conformity to the prevailing value-dissonance), competence (in therapeutically dissipating value-dissonance) and the degree of cognitive assonance of its counselors. This should be an extra-mural function, but unfortunately there exists no agency or professional body anywhere today to discharge it. The fact that the professional psychoanalyst has to undergo analysis himself does not constitute an exception to this assertion. That analysis only serves to make him aware of his own conflicts, but it does not necessarily guarantee their elimination or even reduction. Furthermore, even if we assume that a counselor is completely free of conflict, that is, is wholly cognitive assonant (an obvious impossibility), he may still be value-dissonant for any of the reasons we have previously mentioned. This deficiency of the university counselor is something with which a modern, academic enterprise has to come to terms. There is nothing, however, to prevent the educator who takes the achievement of both cognitive assonance and value-assonance in others (and, we hope, also in himself) as an essential part of his professional duties from dealing with student conflicts. This certainly can be done where there is rapport between teacher and student. Unfortunately we cannot resolve to be between teacher and student. Unfortunately we cannot resolve to be our brother's keeper when it comes to neurotic conflicts and value-dissonance among our colleagues. Professors as a rule do not feel that they need guidance. They generally hold that they are around to dispense it.

Value-dissonance occurs for a variety of other reasons. A subject who furnishes himself an <u>incomplete analysis</u> of the cognitive requirements of a major value in various, possible categories of human action, will create a value pitfall for himself. The educator, of course, is in a very favorable position to complete such an analysis for the student. In fact, I hold this to be one of his singular duties. Value-dissonance also occurs as a result of <u>failure in social perception</u>. If a subject misjudges the nature of a given personal or social context in which he finds himself and then exhibits behavior which is consonant with this misjudgment, it will appear to be value-dissonant to an observer who interprets the same context properly. To reduce value-dissonance in behavior which is a function of social misperception, the educator, it seems to me, should stress for all students the nature and pitfalls of what the phenomenological psychologist calls "the subjective frame of reference." This means that we must emphasize for students that all social perception is to some degree distorted by our own crystallized perceptual and valuational structures, many of which are unexpressed and some of which we are unconscious of. We cannot <u>eliminate</u> the distortion due to social perception, but we can make efforts to minimize it. The only way to minimize such distortion is to encourage subjects pedagogically to check their perceptions against those of others, but these others must be highly selected. They must be individuals who <u>do not</u> share our prepossessions, prejudices and known points of view. Our value opposition must deliberately be singled out. This is in fact not hard to do. However, the disposition for this is weak in most people, who prefer to polarize their frames of reference by consorting only with those with whom they share a common outlook. This troglodytic habit is most pronounced on matters of politics, religion, sex, economics and social issues. To counter it we need a university with the courage to institute tendencious seminars in which students are exposed at given times to representatives of five or six conflicting points of view and who may be bitterly opposed to each other, but who have achieved the skills necessary to woo the intellectual allegiance of others by passionate, but not intolerant, and hostile appeals. In fact, those selected should be the most intelligent representatives of the partisan viewpoints involved. Such meetings should involve a combination of the panel and seminar devices. Given a two hour meeting, panelists should be allowed to go at each other hammer and tongs. During the second hour, students should be allowed a go at the panelists with gloves off. A few semesters of such a procedure may result in having the fur fly, but it will also result in the students developing an awareness of the pitfalls inherent in social misperception and distortion. Above all, it can help to reduce value-dissonance somewhat by developing a deep respect for the practice of correcting the limitations of one's personal frame of reference.

The task of reducing or eliminating value-dissonance in the education of modern man embraces far more than the preceding considerations would lead one to suspect. The value context which characterizes the human predicament involves relationships among values, circumstances and behavior. In order to make clear how wide this context may be, let us designate the present values we hold, the present circumstances we face and the present behavior we exhibit as V_p, C_p, and B_p, respectively; and let us designate the future values toward which we are oriented, the future circumstances and contexts which we hope to usher into being and the future ideal behavior which we hope will characterize man, as V_F, C_F, and B_F, respectively. Then if we permit a somewhat more generalized meaning to the concept of value-dissonance than we have thus far employed, let us note that value-dissonance may occur between any one of the following nine pairs of factors: V_p-V_F, V_p-C_F, V_p-B_F, C_p-V_F, C_p-C_F, C_p-B_F, B_p-V_F, B_p-C_F, and B_p-B_F. By dissonance within any one of these pairs we mean, of course, that one of the present factors, V_p, C_p, or B_p, may block one or more of the future factors in which we are interested. We should also not overlook the possibility that two or three of the present factors may block one or more of the future factors. The types of dissonance with which Festinger and other writers tend to concern themselves are only the blockages or lack of complementarity between any two of the present factors, namely, V_p-C_p, V_p-B_p, and C_p-B_p. These are clearly the dyadic relationships of major importance. However, behavior and values must also be future-oriented. Failure to take stock of consequences is a major form of infantilism described by the psychoanalyst. Here we must note that it is also possible to have an _infantilism of values_. Thus we can see that an education which is fully self-conscious with respect to value, has many byroads and tangents to pursue if it wishes to be given credit for promoting the examined life.

Finally let us note that if we are serious about educating for value, people must be given some idea of the conditions under which the consistency of values _over time_ may constitute a _form of rigidity_. Here the important requirement is to stress the _instrumental nature_ of values. If social circumstances change, a value once appropriate may be dissonant with the new social context. It is in the behavioral and social sciences that the opportunities for bringing out awareness of this type of dissonance are at a maximum. For the intellectually honest educator this area presents the greatest challenge and the greatest opportunity to develop a flexible sense of value. It will also be the area of greatest social resistance, and the educational process in this area will be _maximally disturbing_ to the student. Part of the process of a genuine education, however, is for the subject to have his values challenged so that he is made to reexamine them at maturity. This is the price to be paid if we wish to have an enlightened sense of community. Whether we have the courage to pursue our tasks along these lines remains to be seen. However, the price of refusal or failure is already known. This is the form in which the modern predicament is an expression of Toynbee's "challenge and response." If we do not meet the challenge of making our values cognitively clear to ourselves and if we are indifferent to the need for reducing the value-dissonance in our personal lives and in our own culture, America may become only a memory. If, however, educational leadership rises to the challenge of educating the citizen to the fullest meaning of a sense of value, perhaps we shall live to see a humanistic renaissance in education in which the ancient tradition of demanding that education shall serve to inquire into the nature of the good life may once again come into prominence. A rational self-consciousness about the problem of value is needed more in a technicist society than it was needed in the less sophisticated past. When it comes to asking the question "What is the good life?", the past is always prologue. A philosophy of education limited to the acquisition of only knowledge and skill will, in the end, be self-defeating. A sense of _felt_ values is imperative, and a willingness to translate these into action is more imperative still. This emphasis is well stated in the words of R. G. H. Siu in his The Tao of Science.

The heaping of knowledge needs to be accompanied by a humane polarity. It is the vector quality of learning that determines its social effect. Otherwise, knowledge becomes merely a mass of indeterminate potentialities. Without relevancy, it is an anemic neutrality, that mirage of the pseudo-savant, who gauges his own loftiness by his irresponsibility for the fruits of his actions. To be neutral, after all, is merely to be without association. We may know everything about atoms and molecules; we may be masters of the facts of political science; we may be familiar with all the laws governing human relations; we may memorize all the historical sequences of nations. But if such awareness remains unoriented, how shall we shape our lives? A vital question before educators is therefore: Can their system bestow the necessary vector of human-heartedness? (p. 89)

I am not sanguine over the possibility of developing techniques for creating "human-heartedness." This is not because I believe this attribute is more native than acquired. My doubts may spring more from the fact that communicants of the Western tradition in education have rarely asked themselves what "human-heartedness" is and even more rarely asked for large-scale educational efforts to develop it. More discouraging still is that the intellectual emphasis in Western education has bequeathed us no techniques for imparting a sense of felt value and little interest in examining our values conceptually and in critically trying to ascertain whether our behavior fulfills them. The doubts I have expressed here are the product of past and present trends, and certainly these may be reversed over the course of time. I am, however, genuinely convinced that education can play a role in the reversal of historical trends although this will entail a drastic revamping of our current philosophies of education. If the dedicated and humanistic educator does not take up the torch in the foreseeable future, I know of no one else who will. Of one thing I am sure. If the development of "human-heartedness" does not become one of the basic goals of education and the good life, democracy as a social experiment will fail. If this occurs, it will prove to be the most unnecessary failure in human history.

SOCIAL ZOMBIEISM*–THE ANTI-EXISTENTIAL IN MODERN LIFE

The dictionary defines "zombie" as a supernatural power by which a corpse may be reanimated. Derivatively a "zombie" *is* such a corpse. I wish to maintain in this paper that our *current middlebrow culture* has all the trappings of a supernatural power in that it takes "cultural corpses," metaphorically speaking, namely, our fellow-citizens, and reanimates them through prevailing patterns of motivation. The reanimation is generally short-lived, however, almost invariably disappearing when the incubi of genuine intellectual effort is called for. They are still "corpses," of course, without psychological identity, but they give a semblance of life because of the behavioral and verbal social repertoires to which they have been conditioned. I should like to explore some of the forms which such reanimation takes and to point out, from an existential point of view, the manner in which "zombie behavior" in our time reflects the lack of basic existential concern. The lacks of which I speak are the absence of authenticity of motive, of involvement and commitment and, in general, the absence of "being with others" and "being in the world." These lacks, of course, are not unique to middlebrows. They are a general description of the human condition. They take on, however, special and virulent forms among middlebrows and therefore require an emphasis all by themselves. The "zombie behavior" of which I speak is markedly anti-existential in spirit and perhaps a partial picture of it may prompt a salvageable few to return to authenticity. No single paper can do justice to its myriad forms which occur in such areas as social life, business, education, politics and religion. In this paper I should like

* This phrase was first used by Dr. Jordan M. Scher in a footnote to a paper co-authored with Drs. Geisser and Campaigne in this journal, Vol. 1, No. 4, Winter-Spring 1961, p. 534. The meaning conveyed by it there is similar in part but not wholly identical with that intended by the present paper.

THE JOURNAL OF EXISTENTIAL PSYCHIATRY, Spring 1963 vol. 3, 343-360.

to concentrate on the pandemic expressions of "zombie behavior" only *in the area of social life*. The forms of such behavior in the other areas mentioned merit separate treatment.

The first form of *zombieism* in social life which is of major significance is "rubricization." This is the term employed by Maslow [11] to refer to the habit of looking at one another and assessing one another in terms of labels or stereotypes. In Maslow's own words

Stereotyping is a concept that can apply not only to the social psychology of prejudice, but also to the basic process of perceiving. Perceiving may be something other than the absorption or registration of the intrinsic nature of the real event. It is more often a classifying, ticketing, or labeling of the experience rather than an examination of it, and ought therefore to be called by a name other than true perceiving. What we do in stereotyped or rubricized perceiving is parallel to the use of cliches and hackneyed phrases in speaking.

For instance, it is possible in being introduced to another human being to react to him freshly, to try to understand or to perceive this individual as a unique individual, not quite like anybody else living. More often what we do, however, is to ticket or label or place the man. We place him in a category or a rubric, regard him not as a unique individual, but as an example of some concept or as a representation of a category. For instance, he is a Chinaman, rather than Lum Wang who has dreams and ambitions and fears that are quite different from those of his brother. Or he is labeled as a millionaire or a member of society or a dame or a child or a Jew or a something. In other words, the person engaged in stereotyped perceiving ought to be compared, if we wish to be honest, to a file clerk rather than a camera. The file clerk has a drawer full of folders, and her task is to put every letter on the desk into its appropriate folder under the A's or B's or whatever.

Among the many examples of rubricizing in perceiving, we may cite the tendency to perceive:

1. The familiar and hackneyed rather than the unfamiliar and fresh
2. The schematized and abstract rather than the actual
3. The organized, structured, the univalent rather than the chaotic, unorganized, and ambiguous
4. The named or namable rather than the unnamed and unnamable
5. The meaningful rather than the meaningless
6. The conventional rather than the unconventional
7. The expected rather than the unexpected

Furthermore, where the event is unfamiliar, concrete, ambiguous, unnamed, meaningless, unconventional, or unexpected, we show a strong tendency to twist or force or shape the event into a form that is more familiar, more abstract, more organized, etc. We tend to perceive events more easily as representatives of categories than in their own right, as unique and idiosyncratic. (Pp. 268-9)

Common examples in social life of rubricization occur when the reformer is called a "communist" or when the citizen whose outraged sense of social justice prompts him to action, thereby earns for himself the label of "troublemaker" or "non-cooperative." A still more obvoius example is the individual who shuns certain personalities because of their pettiness or habits of intrigue, thereby earning the monicker of "skizzy," "paranoid," "psychopath," etc. It should not be assumed that a literary familiarity with psychoanalysis is what produces the tendency to employ these last-mentioned gliblabels. The pat use of such rubrics by clinical psychologists on outsiders and even more on one another, is well-known. This has been extensively commented upon by Lynn.[8] Because the clinical psychologist is more interested in Maslow's work than any other variety of psychologist and because Maslow reports that self-actualizing persons are relatively free of the tendency to "rubricize," I feel it pertinent to quote Lynn in this connection.

"Awareness of the damaging effects of being 'clinical' with co-workers led me to make inquiries about this subject of colleagues in a variety of settings. From these inquiries it appears that this practice is widespread and that it seems destructive wherever it is found. By way of illustration a few examples taken from several different settings are presented below.

This first example is that of one clinician in high authority informing another, also in high authority, that a third colleague was 'obviously schizophrenic' and therefore should be dismissed. This 'diagnosis' was made on the basis of a brief interview. The clinician making the evaluation is, paradoxically, quite cautious in clinical practice and makes such diagnoses only after the most careful study. Parenthetically, the 'schizophrenic' colleague has been very productive for a number of years, has published widely, and is still functioning quite well.

A second example is a clinician who seriously passes off anyone who publishes as an 'exhibitionist' and anyone who does research as 'a person who is unable to participate in interpersonal relationships because of his inability to cope with his hostile impulses and must, therefore, withdraw to the cloistered laboratory.'

The third example is that of two clinicians, each of whom informs one in 'strictest confidence' that the other is a 'sick person.'

A final example is that of a psychological study seminar, confounded and reduced to childish insults (in the guise of clinical interpretations) because the participants focus on possible motivational determinants producing their colleagues' ideas rather than on the ideas per se." (pp. 249)

Lynn, himself, points out that the only sensible considerations in being "clinical" with co-workers, is to adopt what he calls a *principle of relevance*. By this he means that a colleague's work should be judged on its merit and not on its presumed dynamics, whether healthy or otherwise. Any personal problems which a colleague is *presumed* to have are irrelevant if they do not affect his work.

Most clinical psychologists are themselves affected by the middle-brow stances all around them. Reinforce a tendency to rubrucize, which is social, with a training to do it richly, and you will find a situation in which categorizing is really running amok.

I am, however, a little ahead of myself. Let us leave the clinical scene. I want to emphasize that middlebrow addiction to labels is not confined to their pejorative use. The habit of slapping down the intellectually gifted and the creative, who tend to remind us of our own mediocrity, by dismissing them with such labels as "aggressive," "too ambitious" and "professional climber" are still further examples but in the opposite direction. By this I mean that the traits being devalued are socially approved, which was not the case for those previously mentioned who, as social critics, rock the boat and make those who accept the status quo meekly most uncomfortable. The important consideration in all these cases, however, is to examine the existential meaning of such rubricization. Essentially it is the intellectually lazy man's device for avoiding thought. Avoiding thought seems to be a national pastime to which such institutions as the cocktail party seem to be perfectly geared. A predilection for rubricization, however, is more than just intellectual laziness. It represents even more significantly an unwillingness to seek to know others in their full, idiosyncratic concreteness. A willingness to do so would be a form of involvement. Unfortunately socially approved forms of alienation encourage the unwillingness which, if properly manifested, will help us to go places. These socially approved forms of alienation encourage us to see others as "on hand" when our paths cross theirs, as "useful and friendly" when they can serve our purposes but, on the other hand, describable by any number of pejorative terms when they appear as a threat or block to our secular ambitions. This *must be* the behavioral repertoire when one's motives are basically egoistic rather than altruistic. Thus if people are seen as means they vary in merit in relation to their potential exploitability and demerit in relation to their frustration potential. A ready-made vocabulary, both honorific and pejorative, is at hand to earmark these differentials in merit and demerit. As a result rubricization has a field day. This tendency is the form which Buber's [2] I-and-It relationship takes when an I-and-Thou relationship has never been developed. A rubric is the perfect device for the "Itness" of the "Other." Studies on perception have revealed the degree to which we fail to notice elements in the ground of a physical figure-ground stable context and the degree to which the inability to lend oneself to the concreteness of elements in the ground, can be reinforced by applying verbal tags to these elements. By a simple parallelism one repeats this operation in *social perception*, the rubric, generally pejorative, being the tag.

There is a singular social phenomenon which operates to reinforce rubricization. It is the capacity for making judgments of others which contravene reality. It operates in both social and working milieus. Examples of what I have in mind occur, for instance, when X is seen as socially boorish, where gossip would have it so, when, as a matter of fact, he is polite, firm, of independent mind and forthright. The label "boorish" will persist for insecure individuals, for the timid, the dependent, the unauthentic and the conformists. Nor does this exhaust the roster of personality syndromes which make of the rubric, a crutch. It will persist for such individuals after they have contacted X again and again even where others, unaffected by a label which they have never heard, state to those who see X through the rubric that he is clearly not boorish to judge from their own contacts. An example in the opposite direction is the tendency to judge Y as intelligent because he carries the label of author, doctor, teacher, civic leader, etc., when Y obviously shows himself to be ignorant, incapable of clarity of thought, intellectually disorganized and irrational in dealing with issues which touch him.

The first rubric is unflattering, the second, laudatory, but the capacity to see their falsity is a function of *disinterested judgment*. Non-disinterested judgment is, of course, a well known example of social self-deception. Social self-deception can take two forms. One is where we lie to ourselves about ourselves. The other is where we lie to ourselves about others. Sartre has given us an existential analysis in depth of the situation in which we lie to ourselves. In his portrait of self-deception, given by Kaufmann,[5] Sartre first distinguishes self-deception from falsehood in that the latter involves lying to others rather than lying to ourselves. He then defines self-deception in the following fashion:

"The situation can not be the same for self-deception if this, as we have said, is indeed a lie to oneself. To be sure, the one who practices self-deception is hiding a displeasing truth or presenting as truth a pleasing untruth. Self-deception then has in appearance the structure of falsehood. Only what changes everything is the fact that in self-deception it is from myself that I am hiding the truth. Thus the duality of the deceiver and the deceived does not exist here. Self-deception on the contrary implies in essence the unity of *a single* consciousness. This does not mean that it can not be conditioned by the "Mit-sein" like all other phenomena of human reality, but the "Mit-sein" can call forth self-deception only by presenting itself as a *situation* which self-deception permits surpassing; self-deception does not come from outside to human reality. One does not undergo his self-deception; one is not infected with it; it is not a *state*. But consciousness affects itself with self-deception. There must be an original intention and a project of self-deception; this project implies a comprehension of self-deception as such and a prereflective apprehension (of) consciousness as affecting itself with self-deception. It follows first that the one to whom the lie is told and the one who lies are one and the same person, which means that I must know in my capacity as deceiver the truth which is hidden from me in my capacity as the one deceived. Better yet I must know the truth very exactly in *order* to conceal it more carefully—and this not at two different moments, which at a pinch would allow us to reestablish a semblance of duality—but in the unitary structure of a single project. How then can the lie subsist if the duality which conditions it is suppressed?" (pp. 243-44)

The point of the quotation is to provide the general structure of self-deception, from an existentialist point of view, for such self-deception is at the bottom of middlebrow social zombieism, not only with respect to rubricizing but even more with respect to middlebrow cultural concerns, as we shall try to show later. The rubric, we repeat, is not the product of disinterested judgment and non-distinterested judgment leads to social self-deception. This social self-deception makes things of other people, struggles erroneously to understand them in terms of *essences* (for after all this is precisely the function of the rubric) and oddly enough "thingifies" people chiefly in terms of pejorative essences. The social zombie thereby brings himself to a state in which persons are noted only as essences, usually unflattering and frequently mistaken. If this process is reinforced by other social zombies, he experiences a sense of aliveness and Mit-sein, wholly synthetic in nature and profoundly in error. The reinforcement provides the corpse with sufficient animation to convince itself it is alive— socially and otherwise.

Sartre's description is general in the selection to which we refer. It provides an existential account of the mechanisms producing self-deception. It does not undertake to separate out the mechanisms by which we lie to ourselves about others from the mechanisms by which we lie to ourselves about ourselves. What then are some of the processes which produce the former type of self-deception?

There are several methods available for succeeding in lying to ourselves about others. One common and obvious method which can be employed to shut out social reality and the reality of others, is to be sloppy in our methods of thinking, communication, evaluation and interpretation. To put it this way, however, is merely to spell out precisely what we mean by that type of intellectual laziness which, as we have already said, is served by rubricization. A second method is one which, I believe, might properly be called "existential irresponsibility." This is the atmosphere which prevails when we simply refuse to avail ourselves of information which is at hand and through which it would be relatively easy to alter one's own phenomenological field. The difference between these two types of escape hatch from the truth, is that the first represents a sin of commission, the second a sin of omission. The commonest form of "existential irresponsibility" is to *see* X via the categorization furnished through the first person who gets our ears. Thereafter this becomes our permanent perceptual set. An exhaustive analysis of the various methods by which we succeed in lying to ourselves about others, is not the intent of the present paper. The core technique, however, *is not* the failure of communication at which we have actually made a stab. It is rather the deliberate effort to avoid any communication at all. We refuse to ask questions of a variety of disinterested persons, we refuse to sit down and talk things over, we insist—especially in a working or professional milieu—that all truth is obtained through the chain of command. Since we have generally built up the chain of command, ourselves, into a tight-knit political machine, we have guaranteed that communication will not take place. The members of such tight-knit political machines have as a basic function to give rubber-stamp approval of the boss's wishes, to find arguments to justify his plans and evaluations and, in general, to serve his purposes, while going through the forms of democratic procedures. We guarantee that we shall hear only what we want to hear. We become prisoners of rigged communication channels in which, through subterfuge and *deception of others,* we deploy our selected cogs to run interference for our wishes and create or sound out reaction. No doubt we invent rationalizations to justify these dishonest and essentially authoritarian procedures. But rationalizations or not, this is a typical way of avoiding communication. Having thus made certain that the cogs of our own selection will reinforce our values and attitudes without necessarily really sharing them, we have smoothed the way for lying to ourselves about others. The herd-minded members of such an organizational pyramid, whether it exists in social, professional or political life, will then always provide the input we want. This closes the circuit and the capacity to lie to ourselves about others is both shared and institutionalized. In addition the situation provides the special dispensation of a permanent morale-builder in which our good judgment is so frequently confirmed that only a "trouble maker" would complain about faulty communication.

A social zombie will believe what he hears and do what he is told to do. Zombie behavior is illustrated in the degree to which we accept gossip—usually liberally developed with rubrics—both socially and in working environments. Gossip is generally listened to uncritically, accepted and acted upon. As we have already remarked, it almost invariably creates what the psychologist calls perceptual set. The fascinating thing about these verbally created perceptual sets is that they are so difficult to dissolve. They are resistant to realities and help to support judgments which contravene them. One often wonders why the social zombie holds on to a perceptual set about X created by gossip, when X is in no relationship to the zombie in question. A little thought, I believe, will indicate the basis for this resistance. First is our tendency to develop vested interests in our own judgments. We become ego-involved. Our self-images become extremely shaky if we are forced to admit to ourselves that we were deeply mistaken in perceiving X in terms of the gossip to which we so readily lent an ear. Instead of building up a self-image with respect to the quality of our judgment, based upon evidence of its soundness in the past (the verification of which would require a type of intellectual effort which goes against the grain of an habitual, intellectual laziness), we look instead for an easy and a cheap acess to *l'amour-propre*. We have to flatter ourselves that we are insightful in having so quickly and intuitively recognized the soundness of the gossip to which we lent so uncritical an ear. Thus we add another dimension to self-deception.

Another singularly important reason we have for accepting and holding on to perceptual sets created by others is the fact that they are our friends. To admit that a friend's judgment is unsound or his motives unjust, is to cast reflection on the soundness of our own judgments in choosing them. Further than this we wish to avoid a type of guilt by association, that is to say, we feel quite consciously that birds of a feather flock together. It then follows that if our friends are individuals of poor judgment and uncharitable motives, it probably indicates the same weakness in ourselves. We cannot bring ourselves to admit these weaknesses. We counter our self-doubts by appropriate rationalizations. From this emerges a further *overdetermination* of our capacity for self-deception.

It is also instructive to note how the social zombie reacts to those rubrics in gossip which are allowed to persist unchecked and unsubstantiated. Highly pejorative rubrics, such as those we have already mentioned, make a man or a woman a *controversial figure*. A controversial figure may be defined in general as a man or a woman who is not easily interchangeable with a representative social zombie. Both in social and professional life a controversial figure is to be avoided, if our own status is to remain unimpaired. Life must run smoothly. Only individuals with no rough edges need apply. These are the social zombies of our time. Individuality and conspicuousness of every sort must be discouraged. The quest for the bland must continue. There is one characteristic way by which controversial figures may be ignored and by which we may guarantee that *nonentities only* receive social or professional acceptance, while permitting the gossip and rubricization concerning controversial figures to go unchecked. We need only develop a sort of social and professional namby-pambyism in which the object is always to look the other way (Good heavens! The gossip and the rubrics might just be both false and unfair, you know) and avoid any honest effort to inquire into their rectitude. Our social and professional attitudes—follies would, of course, be the better word—must be allowed to remain unruffled.

A social or administrative leader is expected to be fertile in developing techniques for avoiding the necessity to face unpleasant issues or unwarranted prejudices squarely. He or she is expected to reduce the motto of the three wise monkeys "See no evil, speak no evil, hear no evil" to "see no evil," only. This leaves everything up in the air where the social zombie feels it should be, since he spends the greater part of his working or leisure time there, himself. A modern Aristophanes would find that the social zombie's version of cloud-cuckooland consists of strenuously developing artifices which help one to avoid social responsibility. The social zombie develops myriad forms of "gentlemen's agreements" to permit the prejudices and rubrics of his friends, cronies and working stooges to diffuse unchecked. He will not permit direct confrontation of an issue. He will not air conflict between associates openly. He will not face the facts—often largely because he does not know how to get at them. Communication is anathema. The welcome receiver of gossip believes that one gets at the facts by gathering as much gossip as possible from as many sources as possible. He believes that from this procedure the truth will emerge on the grounds that it will be somewhere between the contradictory reports which gossip provides. Unfortunately gossip tends to be uniform and homogenized. The administrative zombie and the social zombie seem never to have heard of the sociological principle of the reconvergence of rumor on its own sources thus providing an ersatz and highly untrustworthy but apparent confirmation of its accuracy.

The social zombie is amused and feels quite superior when he reads that mediaeval scholastics used to quarrel about the number of teeth in a horse's mouth. How silly! We do things so much more accurately and efficiently these days. We simply ask the horse's owner!

In social life perhaps the one type of activity which most succinctly betrays social zombieism is our middlebrow effort to play at culture. Whether it is the Civic Cultural Committee, the local PTA lecture circuit, the intellectual light-fantastic of the cocktail party, the cultural katzenjammers of faculty wives or the cultural bosom-heaving of the Ladies' Club, the zombies are animated by a thousand and one substitutes for the genuine life of culture. What the genuine life of culture means has been the subject of a vast literature among which some representative writers are Arnold,[1] Powys,[12] Eliot [4] and Cowell.[3] The familiarity with this literature and, even more, its spirit, is conspicuous by its absence among the devotees of such groups as I have mentioned above. The United States, under the new, middlebrow dispensation, is full of cultural pretensions of a thousand varieties, mostly existential failures. This is so because the characteristic profile of the middlebrow is one in which one never learns to live one's values or even to feel them as something more than cognitive abstractions. The middlebrow's code, a sort of *bushido of retreat*, results in a variety of escape devices most of which require the synthetic forms of animation which convert the cultural corpse into the social zombie of the present. I should like to provide a bill of particulars by merely mentioning these escape devices here without expanding on any of them. They include the sanctification of pretense, role-playing, running along with the herd, life adjustment, cooperation, the attitude of "I don't want to get involved," self-preoccupation, a preference for an irrelevant and bloodless gentility, a malaise in the face of tendentiousness which is regarded as a species of Original Sin and the namby-pambyism to which we have already alluded. On the cultural side the dead hand of zombieism is reflected in a whole pattern of life-denying characteristics which are mistaken for the earmarks of being civilized,* lack of spontaneity in intellectual and aesthetic

* Compare this with the Zen ideal of men who combine strength and gentleness, intelligence and feeling, modesty and self-respect and love of life and other people.

matters (enthusiasm is suspect and is characteristic only of naive and low-class Latins), a consciousness of class shored up by a pronounced xenophobia and cainotophobia, a preference for the passive and the spectator role in all forms of entertainment and a uxoriousness so vast that the male middlebrow probably tips his hat to his wife before he climbs into bed with her.* This all too brief list should not, of course, be taken to be complete. Limitations of space make an exhaustive account of the debits on the cultural balance sheet impossible.

What one can see, however, is that these liabilities are the counterfoils to those psychological stances for which the existentialist pleads— being-in-the-world, seeking authenticity, manifesting *Sorge* or concern, becoming involved and committed, seeking a vital center as a value-orientation, valuing the individual and the unique, distrusting abstractions and respecting the lessons to be learned from concrete individuals and concrete contexts, etc. I am, of course, no authority on middlebrow or mass culture in the sense true of the contributors to such volumes as those prepared by Rosenberg and White,[13] Larrabee and Meyersohn,[6] Lynes [7] and many other specialists on these subjects, too numerous to mention here. But one *does not have to be* to note the social zombieism of middlebrow cultural activities. How does one account for these forms of middlebrow zombieism? There are many explanations which could be furnished. I believe, however, that Macdonald's [9] approach comes closest to a satisfactory explanation.

Macdonald's partial explanation is given in terms of the concept of "homogenization." This refers to the process of refusing to discriminate among values, things or persons with respect to worth and merit. Everything is as interesting as everything else. Everything is no less and no more important than anything else. This is the blandness of namby-pambyism on the cultural front. Any theme is as valuable culturally and educationally as any other. Says Macdonald:

> "*Life* is a typical homogenized magazine, appearing on the mahogany library tables of the rich, the glass cocktail tables of the middleclass, and the oilcloth kitchen tables of the poor. Its

* This class-affiliated habit is mentioned here only because the American middle-class wife is the arbiter of all things cultural in the American middlebrow's home.

contents are as thoroughly homogenized as its circulation. The same issue will present a serious exposition of atomic energy followed by a disquisition on Rita Hayworth's love life; photos of starving children picking garbage in Calcutta and of sleek models wearing adhesive brassieres; an editorial hailing Bertrand Russell's eightieth birthday (A GREAT MIND IS STILL ANNOYING AND ADORNING OUR AGE) across from a full-page photo of a matron arguing with a baseball umpire (MOM GETS THUMB); nine color pages of Renoir paintings followed by a picture of a roller-skating horse; a cover announcing in the same size type two features: A NEW FOREIGN POLICY, BY JOHN FOSTER DULLES and KERINA: HER MARATHON KISS IS A MOVIE SENSATION. Somehow these scramblings together seem to work all one way, degrading the serious rather than elevating the frivolous. Defenders of our Masscult society like Professor Edward Shils of the University of Chicago—he is, of course, a sociologist—see phenomena like *Life* as inspiriting attempts at popular education—just think, nine pages of Renoirs! But that roller-skating horse comes along, and the final impression is that both Renoir and the horse were talented." (pp. 12-13.)

I cannot refrain from separately furnishing a footnote to the preceding quotation, which Macdonald tagged on to it.

"The advertisements provide even more scope for the editors' homogenizing talents, as when a full-page photo of a ragged Bolivian peon grinningly drunk on coca leaves (which Mr. Luce's conscientious reporters tell us he chews to narcotize his chronic hunger pains) appears opposite an ad of a pretty, smiling, well dressed American mother with her two pretty-smiling-well dressed children (a boy and a girl, of course—children are always homogenized in our ads) looking raptly at a clown on a TV set, the whole captioned in type big enough to announce the Second Coming: RCA VICTOR BRINGS YOU A NEW KIND OF TELEVISION—SUPER SETS

WITH "PICTURE POWER." The peon would doubtless find the juxtaposition piquant if he could afford a copy of *Life*, which, luckily for the Good Neighbor Policy, he cannot."

With respect to Henry Luce's encouragement of the production of cultural homogenization, let us note that Macdonald ought to know something about Henry, since he wrote for *Fortune* for several years, resigning only when he felt that his pieces were being bowdlerized by the editor of that publication.* I also suspect to judge from pieces which have appeared on the subject, Henry's wife, Claire Booth Luce has been influential in encouraging the homogenization of *Life* magazine. No doubt this is because her thinking is Booth Luce and not Claire!

Now my point in the present context is that Macdonald's concept of homogenization is an apt description of the end-process of psychological and cultural failure among middlebrow zombies. His description, however, does not furnish an existential account of the motivation dynamics which produce this terminal homogenization. It is true that *Life's* fare is as painless and strainless as a cocktail-party gambit. It enables one to deal with culture in the manner of a bus-driver and his family surveying the exhibits in the Metropolitan Museum of Art on his day off. A somewhat better parallel is the radio announcer discussing a flood in a downtown sewer with the same gravity and flatness of voice with which he announces that China has just poured troops into North Korea. And perhaps an even better parallel is the newsreel which furnishes the news of the world—five minutes display of the Army-Navy big football game and one minute devoted to the fighting around Dienbienphu. Underlying all these equalities of insensitivity and obtuseness is precisely the inability to work through the merits of the ideas played with, the art materials viewed and experienced, the values invoked. More than superficiality is involved. There is a failure of what might be called "cultural empathy." The authenticity and being of significant events and artistic

* See pp. 8-9 of the Introduction: Politics Past in Macdonald's *Memoirs Of A Revolutionist*, New York: Meridian Books, Inc. 1957, Pp. 376, for an account of Macdonald's sojourn on *Fortune*.

experiences, the deep and complete meaning of difficult ideas and the intent of what should be directing values, are all lost. They do not become part of the warp and woof of one's own, inner being. Without these contacts in depth culture is rootless. Without such contacts in depth its forms and themes are dead for us and, if so, they have to be looked at in terms of lifeless stereotypes, meaningless catch phrases and flimsy shells of meaning. The proper stance then for a middlebrow mortician performing a cultural necropsy would be to assume a cadaver-like stillness in the presence of his fellows when they play at culture. This would, of course, not be well received among middle-brows. A cocktail party would then begin to take on too much the semblance of a morgue and so a "dance of the cadavers" is provided. The social zombies display an ersatz animation over cultural themes, trying to infuse them with a spirit they do not comprehend, a stimulation they do not feel and a concern they do not have. In this effort at animated infusion one has the cultural form of social zombieism. Unfortunately, spiritually, intellectually, psychologically and aesthetically, it is not an example of innocuous desuetude.

The conclusions to be drawn, I believe, are fairly clear. What I have called social zombieism in middleclass culture can occur only because of its denial of depth in human relations, its unconcern for the I-And-Thou of the social covenant, its retreat from the existentially concrete and unique, and its expectation that in the realm of values one can get something for nothing. The incomprehending blight of social zombieism is its persistent delight in spiritual inflation and its tendency to create alienation in everything it touches. Its major folly is the worship of form without substance or spirit. It advocates disengagement from life and succeeds in achieving it. It accepts social irresponsibility and perhaps it needs to be lambasted for that irresponsibility as MacLeish [10] lambasted the intellectuals of the 30's for it in a by-now famous piece. The life-space and lived time of those zombies who call themselves people and who mistake the shadows of culture and social relations for their substance, is so vastly different from a healthy existentialist consciousness, that the reclamation and salvaging of middlebrows will have to involve a special form of existential psychiatry. If one can guess at the type of therapy which would have saved Tolstoi's [14] Ivan Ilych, then perhaps one can guess what might be used to set middlebrow consciousness on the right road to psychological and cultural health. I shall not venture a guess, myself, much as I recognize how serious a disease social zombieism is in our time. I hope, however, that workers in the field of existential psychiatry will come up with something before twentieth century social zombieism bequeaths us a vast, middlebrow, cultural graveyard. Whom the Gods destroy, they first make mad!

REFERENCES

1. Arnold, Matthew. *Culture and Anarchy. An Essay In Political & Social Criticism.* Cambridge: Cambridge University Press. 1957. Pp. 241

2. Buber, Martin. *I and Thou.* New York: Charles Scribner's Sons, 1957. Pp. 137

3. Cowell, F. R. *Culture In Private And Public Life.* New York: Frederick A. Praeger, 1959. Pp. 357

4. Eliot, T. S. *Notes towards the Definition Of Culture.* New York: Harcourt, Brace, 1949. Pp. 128

5. Kaufmann, Walter (Editor). *Existentialism from Dostoevsky to Sartre.* New York: Meridian Books, 1956. Pp. 319

6. Larrabee, Eric and Meyersohn, Rolf (Editors). *Mass Leisure.* Glencoe, Illinois: The Free Press, 1958. Pp. 429

7. Lynes, Russell. *The Tastemakers.* New York: Harper, 1949. Pp. 362

8. Lynn, David B. On Being "Clinical" with Colleages. *The American Psychologist.* Vol. II, No. 5, May, 1956. Pp. 249-50.

9. Macdonald, Dwight. Masscult & Midcult. New York: *Partisan Review* (distributed by Random House). 1961. Pp. 78.

10. MacLeish, Archibald. The Irresponsibles. In *The Intellectuals, A Controversial Portrait.* Edited by Huszar, George B. de Glencoe, Illinois: The Free Press, 1960. Pp. 543

11. Maslow, Abraham H. *Motivation and Personality.* New York: Harper, 1954. Pp. 411

12. Powys, John Cowper. *The Meaning Of Culture.* New York: W. W. Norton, 1929. Pp. 275

13. Rosenberg, Bernard, and White, David Manning (Editors). *Mass Culture. The Popular Arts In America.* Glencoe, Illinois: The Free Press & The Falcon's Wing Press, 1957. Pp. 561

14. Tolstoi, Leo. The Death of Ivan Ilych. *In Quintet.* New York: Pyramid Books, 1956. Pp. 287

Dr. Henry Winthrop is professor in the Department Of Interdisciplinary Social Sciences, University Of South Florida. He organized
the curriculum of that department and served as its chairman from
1964-1967, inclusive.

He has taught at several institutions. Prior to teaching he worked
as an economist with the Federal Government and New York State.
During this period he conducted research in the areas of productiv-
ity and technological studies, input-output studies of industries,
and mathematical and economic studies of proposed, new legislation
for low and medium cost housing.

Dr. Winthrop has authored some 500-600 publications, consisting of
papers in psychology, sociology and economics, governmental studies
and reports, and monographs and chapters contributed to edited volumes. In 1968 he published Ventures In Social Interpretation, part
of the Sociology Series of Appleton-Century-Crofts, Inc.

His published work in the behavioral and social sciences includes
contributions to such areas as the following: social policy and planning, constitutional psychology, communication, the measurement of
attitude-consistency, humanistic psychology, community development,
mathematical models of behavioral diffusion theory, mass culture and
mass leisure, the social impacts of science and technology and studies
of the future. The present volume organizes a sample of papers that
deal with the importance and the value of the humanistic viewpoint in
the social and behavioral sciences.

The author is presently on the editorial boards of more than a dozen,
professional journals several of which are in the behavioral and social sciences. He has also received honorary appointments both to
advisory bodies of international organizations devoted to interdisciplinary effort in the social sciences and other areas and to international groups devoted to projects for world government and world
peace.

Education: B.S., 1935 (C.C.N.Y); M.A., 1940 (George Washington University); and Ph.D., 1953 (The New School For Social Research). Other
schools attended: Brooklyn Polytechnic Institute, Graduate School of
the Department of Agriculture and American University.